A revelation for the times we live in

Final Harvest

Trisha

THE FULFILLMENT OF THE
EXTRAORDINARY APPARITIONS
OF THE BLESSED VIRGIN MARY
AT MEDJUGORJE

Wayne Weible

Author of the International Bestseller
Medjugorje: The Message,

and other books on the
apparitions at Medjugorje

Final Harvest
By
Wayne Weible

ISBN 1-891280-47-3

Library of Congress Cataloging in Publication Date.

Publisher:
CMJ Marian Publishers
Post Office Box 661
Oak Lawn, Illinois 60454
www.cmjbooks.com
jwby@aol.com

Graphic Design: Lisa Duffy

Editorial Assistance: Cynthia Nicolosi

Printed in the United States of America.

Acknowledgments

The messages here related that have been given in apparition by the Blessed Virgin Mary at Medjugorje have been obtained and verified from a wide variety of qualified sources, the most important being personal contacts and interviews with the visionaries, priests, and others involved. All of the messages come under strict theological scrutiny by the priests in charge of the parish of Saint James Catholic Church in Medjugorje to assure they are in total compliance with Scripture and the doctrines of the Catholic Church. If any message, event, or activity originating in the apparitions were not in conformity with this time-tested formula, the Church would condemn the phenomena immediately. After more than twenty years of daily encounters with the Blessed Virgin, no such condemnation has occurred.

The wording and grammar of the messages are subject to the variance of translation from the Croatian language into English. No attempt is made here to grammatically correct or alter any part of the messages so as to retain their original flavor. Virtually all are given in the full text as they were received. They appear in italic type throughout the book; any emphasis added to them by the author is duly noted.

All scriptural references are taken from the Revised Standard Version of the Bible.

The author acknowledges that the final determination of the authenticity of the apparitions at Medjugorje rests with the Catholic Church and submits entirely to its final conclusion. However, given the thorough investigations already conducted by theological, scientific, and medical experts, in addition to the abundant spiritual fruits, I accept the apparitions as authentic until final judgment is rendered. They are addressed as such in this book.

This book is dedicated to people of all faiths who hear the messages of God and attempt to live them.

Table of Contents

PART IV
Storm

PART V
The Harvest

Preface to the Revised Edition

Final Harvest is a greatly revised and updated edition of my last book *The Final Harvest: Medjugorje at the End of the Century.* The new release, with a new publishing house, CMJ Marian Publishers, brings the story of the incredible apparitions of the Blessed Virgin Mary in the rural village of Medjugorje in Bosnia-Hercegovina right up to the present year of 2002. In many ways, it is a new book.

Several factors contributed to the revision of this work, notably, the release of the so-called "third" secret of Fatima, and the need to bring into perspective the dramatic events of September 11, 2001. The final harvest has never seemed so close. It is imperative to understand the signs of the times and heed the messages that the Blessed Virgin has brought us, not once, but many times.

With this in mind, the revision of my original manuscript gives me the opportunity to further expound on what I see as a vital connection between Medjugorje and its two most important forerunners: La Salette and Fatima. In particular, the content of the "third" Fatima secret—and, in fact, the whole of the Fatima message—is, in my opinion, strongly tied to the events and messages of Medjugorje. We may speak of Medjugorje as the *fulfillment* of Fatima. Such a conclusion has been affirmed by Lucia herself. It is further supported by the astounding revelations made in a nearly parallel time period to Father Stefano Gobbi of the Marian Movement of Priests.

I hope those of you who read the original work will find the revisions and updates in *Final Harvest* worth the extra effort of reading it again. I truly think you will. Those who are just learning about the apparitions of the Blessed Virgin Mary at Medjugorje have the latest and most up-to-date book on what I consider to be the most important event of our time.

Wayne Weible, March 25, 2002

Prologue

The Most Important Event of Our Time

For more than twenty years, the Blessed Virgin Mary has reportedly appeared daily in the rural village of Medjugorje in Bosnia-Hercegovina. This unprecedented series of apparitions to six youths began in June 1981 and continues to the present. The purported objective of this remarkable event is to bring the people of the world back to God. The apparitions are elevated in drama and urgency as the Virgin reveals that these will be her final apparitions on earth because, as she adds, *It will no longer be necessary* . . .

In the 2000-year history of the Catholic Church, the Blessed Virgin Mary has appeared in apparition many times. The most notable sites of past apparitions are Guadalupe, in Mexico (1531); Rue du Bac, in Paris, France (1830); La Salette (1846) and Lourdes (1858), also in France; and, the most well-known before Medjugorje, Fatima, in Portugal (1917). But never has the Blessed Virgin Mary appeared daily for so long a period of time, to so many chosen visionaries, with such profound global impact, as she has at Medjugorje. She has made her purpose clear in her messages: in this, her last visit to the earth, she issues a familiar but urgent and repeated call for the world to turn to God for true peace and happiness.

The messages of Medjugorje represent a culmination of all that has come before. Their specific theme was initialized in the single revelation made at La Salette; it was highlighted and made even more explicit during the apparitions at Fatima. It finds further corroboration in a startling series of inner locutions given to an Italian Franciscan priest by the name of Father Stefano Gobbi during a nearly parallel time period. Given the consistency and coherency of these heavenly messages over a wide expanse of years, we cannot help but draw the conclusion that Medjugorje is a major part of heaven's final harvest of souls. It is, in my opinion, the historic conclusion of all previous Marian apparitions—the most important event of our time.

In the summer of 1981, when the Medjugorje apparitions began, the village of Medjugorje, and the Federation of Yugoslavia in which it was located, poignantly represented a microcosm of the modern world plagued by social injustice and the threat of war. For centuries, this Eastern European region had been ripped apart by the mutual antagonisms of its three distinct ethnic groups: Croatians, Serbians and Muslims. The region's history had been one of "no peace." Every succeeding generation suffered from an endless cycle of invasion, resistance, and liberation. In between periods of conquest by outsiders, natives practiced war on each other. Hate-filled, reciprocating atrocities were only quelled following World War II through the forced unity of an atheistic, Marxist dictatorship: the Federation of Yugoslavia.

Despite the miracle of the Blessed Virgin's apparitions in this region, the people as a whole did not initially heed the call to reconciliation. Croat and Serb could not live with each other; neither could stand the converted Muslim Slav, created out of four centuries of Turkish rule. Still, the Blessed Virgin continued to appear daily to six chosen teenagers in the small village—even throughout the period of a bloody, devastating, three-year civil war begun in 1991.

Incredibly, pilgrims came from all over the world even during the height of the active conflict. They came not just for private, spiritual reasons, but to bring desperately needed material aid to hapless victims. Among the pilgrims were those who had previously been to Medjugorje on pilgrimage; now, they returned without regard to personal danger or death. This response by ordinary people to the Medjugorje messages serves as powerful evidence of the good seed of spiritual conversion that falls into fertile soil and gives off a hundred-fold.

The Blessed Virgin appears to Catholic youths in Medjugorje, and her messages often ask adherence to the sacraments of the Roman Catholic Church. However, she has made clear from the beginning that her messages are for people of all beliefs. This is confirmed by the large number of non-Catholics who have been transformed spiritually by the messages of the apparitions. That includes the author of this book.

My purpose here is not just to tell the story or provide authenticated proof of the supernatural source of the apparitions at Medjugorje. Rather, I wish to present the *spiritual* story of Medjugorje: its connection to other Marian apparitions, and its impact on individuals. The messages themselves provide the framework around which I will weave factual details, stories, and personal commentary gleaned from more than sixteen years of personal involvement and investigation. These elements lend witness far better than reams of facts, theology, and debate.

Without sounding a frantic or apocalyptic note, I also hope to show the relevance of Medjugorje to these times by connecting this event to the Blessed Virgin's previous appearances at La Salette and Fatima, as well as the locutions she has given to Father Stefano Gobbi of the Marian Movement of Priests. The activity of the Blessed Virgin Mary in the last two centuries, culminating in her on-going presence in Medjugorje, is a remarkable, thought-provoking reality of our age. What she started at La Salette, she amplified at Fatima and confirmed through the Marian Movement of Priests. She lives it daily with the whole world through the apparitions given at Medjugorje. The primary message of all these events is that the final harvest of souls is a harvest of love and mercy—not of gloom and doom. The Blessed Virgin tells us that at the conclusion of the Medjugorje apparitions, the world will undergo a spiritual cleansing that will mark the beginning of an unprecedented era of peace through a full return to God. It unequivocally does not mean that this is the end of the physical world.

While there will be much of an apocalyptic nature to relate in these pages, it is the good fruits of the Medjugorje apparitions discovered by people of all faiths—and those with no faith—that this book desires to reveal to the reader. My objective is the spiritual renewal and strengthening of individuals reading about the apparitions of the Blessed Virgin Mary at Medjugorje for the first time, as well as those already familiar with them.

My hope is that this book will leave every reader wanting to be among the souls of the final harvest.

PART 1

Preparation

*I want you to know, brethren, that I have often
intended to come to you . . . in order that I may
reap some harvest among you as well as among
the rest of the Gentiles. I am under obligation
both to Greeks and to barbarians, both to the
wise and to the foolish.*

Romans 1:13-14.

Chapter 1

Preparing the Way

The young Franciscan priest from Bosnia-Hercegovina stared blankly out the window as the plane approached the airport. It was the first week of May 1981, and the Italian weather was near perfect. He should have felt the joyful anticipation of attending a conference of the Catholic Charismatic Renewal in Rome. At the moment, however, he only hoped the conference would rekindle within him the flame of the Holy Spirit that had so strongly marked his brief priesthood and had, of late, been somewhat dimmed by circumstances.

The apathy of the people in his parish, not to mention the surrounding parishes, had brought Father Tomislav Vlasic to a discouraging point. He had first come to his assignment at Saint Francis of Assisi Catholic Church in Capljina filled with a fervor well expressed through a strong gift of preaching and a magnetic personality. As a result, the young priest had been invited to nearby villages to preach the gospel message. Instead of conversions, he was met with indifference. Many young people did not attend Mass; work on Sundays was the norm. Families praying together seemed to be a thing of the past.

Father Tomislav came to the conference with one thought in mind: to seek help through the wisdom of two well-known members of the charismatic movement who would both be speakers ·at the conference. Sister Briege McKenna, an Irish nun living in the United States, was well known for her strong gift of prophecy and healing ministry, particularly with priests. Father Emiliano Tardif, a French-Canadian presently stationed in Colombia, South America, also enjoyed the charism of a healing ministry. Father Tomislav wanted them both to pray over him in the hope of restoring his spiritual buoyancy and overcoming the resistance of the people at home.

Father Tomislav's prayers were answered in a way far beyond his expectations. As she prayed over him, Sister Briege began

3

describing a vivid, prophetic vision, telling him that she "saw him in a twin-towered church sitting in a chair and surrounded by a great crowd." There were streams of water flowing from beneath the chair out onto the people, she related, "streams of powerful healing water . . ."

Father Tomislav was deeply touched by the vision, but also bewildered. The only church he knew with twin towers was twelve miles away in the parish of Medjugorje. But he was happy, having received far more than anticipated through the encounter with Sister Briege. Surely, this was a sign that the people were finally going to respond to his ministry.

What occurred next raised his spirits well above mere happiness, even though the young priest was not quite certain of what it meant. The following day, Father Tardif came to him. After praying over Father Tomislav, he took him aside, embraced him, and said, "My dear young friend, I have a wonderful message for you from Jesus. He says: 'Don't worry, I am sending you my mother!'"

. . . .

The old woman groaned as she straightened from a long period of bending over to prune the young tobacco plants. She wiped her brow and glanced down the row of plants where an equally aged companion doing the same task worked her way towards her. It was mid-morning in early May 1981, yet another hard day of work in one of the tobacco fields that dotted the landscape of the village of Medjugorje. The weathered faces of the women bore evidence of years of such labor.

The monotony and physical stress of the women's work was offset by their constant praying of the rosary in a steady, low-pitched monotone as they made their way toward each other. This mixing of labor and devout prayer was a way of life among the older women of the village and had been so for generations.

Suddenly, the woman stopped still and stared. She shook her head, rubbed her eyes and looked again. There, in a clear vision out of a flash of light, floating eerily in her direction above the row of tobacco plants, was what appeared to be an ancient chariot drawn by two white horses. It moved steadily but silently, slowly passing over her. As it did, she saw that the chariot contained a very old man with long white hair and beard. The vision then slowly faded as the woman, sensing something spiritual in the mysterious phenomenon, acknowledged what her eyes had seen by reverently making the sign of the cross. She then numbly returned to her work.

When she met her companion in the middle of the row, they paused and looked at each other. Hesitatingly, the woman gestured in the direction where the vision had faded away and asked, "Did you see—?"

"Yes," her companion answered in a whisper, nodding slowly, "yes, I saw it."

After an extended silence, each again made the sign of the cross and resumed working the tobacco plants.

Several weeks later, in the parish of Medjugorje, with its twin-towered Saint James Church, the image of a beautiful young woman identifying herself as the Blessed Virgin Mary made her first appearance on a hillside to six Croatian youths. It was the first of what would become daily supernatural apparitions that would take the village, the region, and eventually the entire world to unprecedented spiritual heights—well past the wildest dreams of Father Tomislav.

By no mere coincidence, the most dazzling and powerful apparitions of the Blessed Virgin Mary in history began on the 24th day of June, recognized in the Roman Catholic Church as the Feast Day of Saint John the Baptist, the great precursor of Christ.

. . . . .

And the disciples asked him, "Then why do the scribes say that first Elijah must come?" He replied, "Elijah does come, and he is to restore all things; but I tell you that Elijah has already come, and they did not know him, but did to him whatever they pleased. So also the Son of man will suffer at their hands." Then the disciples understood that he was speaking to them of John the Baptist.
Matthew 17:10-13

Chapter 2

The Miracle

On June 24, 1981, the figure of a young woman in a shimmering brilliance of light smiled at the six youths kneeling before her on the little hill overlooking the village of Medjugorje. She then slowly raised her arms, smiled, and softly said to them: Praise be Jesus!

Twenty-one years later, the young woman, early on identified as the Blessed Virgin Mary, is still appearing at Medjugorje—as she has each day during this time. On June 25, 2001, more than 100,000 people from nations around the world gathered in the village to commemorate the event. Each daily encounter, including this one, has started with the same greeting, Praise be Jesus! The greeting itself serves as confirmation that the apparitions are a gift of grace from heaven, a grace that has spread steadily throughout the world.

Not surprisingly, the message given to the millions of followers on the 20th anniversary of the apparitions was in essence a summation of the Blessed Virgin's many messages over the years in Medjugorje: *Dear children, I am with you and I bless you with all my motherly blessing. Especially today when God gives you abundant graces pray and seek God through me. God gives you great graces; that is why, little children, make good use of this time of grace and come closer to my heart so that I can lead you to my Son Jesus. Thank you for your response to my call.*

. . . . .

The apparitions actually started on June 24, 1981, when a startled teenager, fifteen-year-old Ivanka Ivankovic, was the first to see the vision. She was soon joined by several of her peers. The figure of a young woman, bathed in an unearthly light and hovering about fifty yards up the side of a small hill near the village, smiled continuously and held an infant in her arms as she beckoned the youths to come to her. From a strong Catholic upbringing, the

6

young people immediately recognized the woman as the Blessed Virgin Mary.

But they were too frightened to respond, frozen in place by fear, some praying and some weeping. One of the boys, Ivan Dragicevic, sixteen, took one look and ran away. As a light mist of rain began to fall, the others slowly backed away from the scene, then turned and swiftly ran to their homes where they excitedly told family and friends what had happened. News spread through the small community like wild fire: "Gospa"[1] had appeared in their village!

The following evening, June 25, the youths who had seen the vision the previous day felt an irresistible inner urge to return to the scene. Again, the figure appeared, this time without the infant in her arms, whom she would later identify as the baby Jesus. When she beckoned to them, the young people raced up the side of the bramble-covered, rocky slopes at a speed normally beyond their physical ability. It was a climb that usually took twelve to fifteen minutes, but they did it in only two. Kneeling less than five feet away, Ivanka and Ivan were joined by Mirjana Dragicevic, 15, Marija Pavlovic, 16, Vicka Invankovic, 17, and Jakov Colo, only 10.

Within minutes, fear gave way to youthful curiosity, and questions poured forth: Who are you? Why have you come? What do you want? The figure in the light, after identifying herself as the Blessed Virgin Mary, told them, I have come to tell you that God exists and that He loves you. *I have come because there are many true believers here. I wish to be with you to convert and to reconcile the whole world.*

The children stared in awe. Mirjana, who with Ivanka had been the first to see the Blessed Virgin, then asked, "Why are you appearing to us? We are no better than others." The Virgin smiled and paused before answering, I do not necessarily choose the best [people].

It was a telling response. On the previous evening, Ivanka and Mirjana, having finished evening chores, slipped off to a secluded

---

1. An affectionate, Croatian term for the Blessed Virgin Mary.

spot to listen to rock music while smoking cigarettes pilfered from their fathers. This venial act of experimentation would serve as example to millions who would later journey to Medjugorje on pilgrimage that God chooses ordinary people for extraordinary missions. Those chosen for a charism that allows them to see a heavenly visitor are chosen not necessarily because of the good they may have done, but for the good they can do.

This first apparition of the Blessed Virgin Mary with conversation lasted for what seemed a long time to the children; they didn't want it to end, but they were too awed to ask more questions. One of them finally asked: "Will you come back?" Yes, the Virgin responded, *to the same place as yesterday.*

A small crowd of local villagers witnessed the entire scene. They had come to the site on this second day as word had spread quickly that the children were claiming to have seen the Blessed Virgin on the hill. Few had believed them, including family members. Vicka's sister playfully asked her if maybe she had seen a flying saucer, while Marija laughed at first when an uncle teased her sister Milka, who had briefly seen the Madonna with Ivanka and Mirjana on the first day. Now, on this second day, Marija was there in place of her sister who, much to her distress, was made to tend to the family sheep. At Marija's side was little Jakov who had been visiting her home when Ivanka came in looking for Milka and shouting excitedly that the Virgin was appearing again.

By the third day, Friday, June 26, the entire region was abuzz with excitement over the reported apparitions. As the six youths knelt again in a state of ecstasy, a crowd estimated at near three thousand reacted. Emotion-driven confusion soon reigned. Vicka's grandmother had told her to take holy water to sprinkle on the vision if it appeared again. This was a test, an age-old test of faith for the villagers, to make sure that a spiritual visitor was from God. Vicka literally threw the entire contents of the bottle on the figure, saying, "If you are not from God, go away!" In response, the Blessed Virgin smiled radiantly, pleased with the test.

What happened next explained the purpose of the Virgin's visit and the choice of this specific site.

As the apparition ended, the visionaries were separated from each other as villagers tugged at them and begged for details of their encounter. Marija, alone, made her way down the pathway of Podbrdo Hill. All at once, she felt a mysterious tug that moved her to the side of the trail where suddenly the Virgin appeared to her again. The radiant happiness of the beautiful young woman surrounded by light was now transformed into somber concern. She hovered in front of the image of an empty, rainbow-colored cross, tears pouring down her cheeks as she pleaded: *Peace, Peace, Peace! Be reconciled! Only Peace! Make your peace with God and among yourselves. For that, it is necessary to believe, to pray, to fast, and to go to confession.*

It was an impassioned warning that would be repeated over and over again in the succeeding days, months, and years. This second message, on that first day of intimate conversation with the Mother of God, was a pointed warning not only to the three ethnic groups that formed the population of Yugoslavia, but most emphatically, to the whole world.

. . . . .

And a great portent appeared in heaven, a woman clothed with the sun, with the moon under her feet, and on her head a crown of twelve stars . . . Revelation 12:1

Chapter 3

The Harvest Begins

At the time when the apparitions began, the world was ablaze with excessive nationalistic fervor as even the smallest ethnic entity fought fiercely for independence and pride. Today, it is the same, if not worse. Historically, the fruit of such poison has been bloodshed of the innocent while the strong struggle for control, driven by the twin motivators of power and greed. Such was the stage setting of this incredible miracle that would begin a harvest of souls for God.

When she appeared on the hill that first evening, holding the infant Jesus in her arms, the Blessed Virgin was, in a way, renewing the birth of the Son of God in a village which very much resembled Bethlehem. She emphasized in her initial messages that she came seeking the only true peace for the world, and specifically, for that region.

Yet even with the impact of such a miracle, the people, including church leaders of the three ethnic groups, would largely ignore her early warning call for reconciliation among them. The tantalizing lure for immediate prestige and power overwhelmed the bleak promise of long-suffering peace. Ten years later, the result of ignoring the Virgin's plea for reconciliation would be a devastating, horror-filled war, leaving the republics comprising former Yugoslavia free from the bonds of Communism, but in shambles. It would be yet another of the world's countless rejections of heaven's grace to give true peace through the birth, crucifixion, and resurrection of Jesus Christ.

But for the moment, the awesome reality of the Virgin's apparitions created for the masses an emotional atmosphere of repentance, conversion, and unlimited hope. Surprising the visionaries, not to mention the local church hierarchy, the apparitions continued daily with no sign of stopping. Startling messages were given, and crowds swelled as people streamed in from the surrounding area.

Then came an incredible revelation, incredible as much for its content as its meaning. Visionary Ivanka's mother had died just a month before the apparitions began. She had been rushed to the hospital in the nearby city of Mostar with a serious illness, but no one expected her death. Her daughter was left lonely and depressed. Now, the young girl was on the hill overlooking her home, able to see and converse with a beautiful lady who claimed to be from heaven. Her question was inevitable: "Dear Lady, where is my mother?"

The Virgin's answer filled the young girl with unbounded joy: *Your mother is in heaven with us!*

It was astounding news that reverberated through the village and surrounding communities. People wondered, how could this woman go straight to heaven when she had done nothing particularly special in life? The answer was simple. She had been a good wife and mother and had lived her faith daily with prayers and frequent attendance at Mass, accepting what God had given her in life and fulfilling the responsibility that came with it. The Blessed Virgin would emphasize these basic requirements for holiness through her ensuing messages.

By now, however reluctant, the local church was becoming involved. Initial reaction to the youths' claims of seeing the Madonna daily ranged from total rejection to calls for exorcism. Cautious and even skeptical Franciscan priests urged the visionaries to request a sign from the Virgin to prove that the apparitions were really from God. Her response was calm and direct: *Blessed are those who have not seen and who believe.*

Many priests remained skeptical. The young visionaries were questioned sharply in long sessions with the Franciscans. Worse was the interrogation by the local Communist authorities. The children were accused of drug use, of being mentally disturbed, or of just plain lying. Some thought it was a prank that had gotten out of hand, or a deliberate hoax perpetrated by the Franciscans themselves. Through it all, the six youths remained steadfast. In the face of questioning by all camps, they stated repeatedly that they had seen and were continuing to see the Virgin each evening. No threats against them or their families could sway them from this claim.

Within weeks, thousands were coming to the village for the daily apparition. A pattern was soon established: following a period of prayer led by the visionaries, the Blessed Virgin would appear to the children after three sudden bursts of a brilliant light that was sometimes visible to a few in the crowd. The visionaries would then fall to their knees in synchronization after stopping their prayers on exactly the same word, sometimes even on the same syllable, and stare at the spot where the Virgin was evidently appearing. Each visionary would seem to be in conversation with her, separate from the others. Their mouths moved to form words but without audible sound to the onlookers.

The apparition, always close to the same time each evening, would last for various periods of time ranging from a few minutes to an hour. It depended, the visionaries explained, on the needs presented and the teachings of the Virgin during the time of the apparition. Afterwards, the visionaries would describe the experience to the people, including what the Virgin looked like.

They saw her in a three-dimensional way, just as we see each other, they would explain. She was described as looking very Croatian,[2] about nineteen to twenty-one years of age, approximately 5'7" tall, slender in form, and indescribably beautiful beyond any statue or picture they had ever seen. She had blue eyes, a pale ivory white complexion, with a small curl of black hair showing on the left side of her face from under a long white veil that reached down in length to a small white cloud that covered her feet. The cloud, the children stated, grew with the length of time the Virgin remained in apparition. Her dress was described as long, without a sash, and of a lucent, silver-gray color. And, they added, she had a crown of twelve stars circling her head.[3]

Podbrdo Hill, once a secluded pasture for the sheep of the villagers, was now covered daily with people. Relatives brought the

2. It is not unusual that the Blessed Virgin Mary appears Croatian to the visionaries at Medjugorje since the village is predominantly Croatian. Historically, she appears as a woman or young girl of the nationality of the country where the apparition is occurring, underlining her role as spiritual mother of all people.

3. The Blessed Virgin Mary is described as having a crown of twelve stars in Revelation 12:1: "And a great portent appeared in heaven, a woman clothed with the sun, with the moon under her feet, and on her head a crown of twelve stars . . ."

sick and handicapped, begging the visionaries to ask Gospa's intercession for a healing. The parents of one handicapped child asked the visionaries to intercede on his behalf. The little boy could neither hear nor speak, and he walked with a limp. The question was put to the Virgin and she answered after looking at the little boy and his family for a long time: *Have them believe strongly in his cure. Go in the peace of God.*

Incredibly, the parents were disappointed in the answer. They had expected immediate healing for their child. The Virgin Mary was telling them to pray, have faith and trust. But they obeyed. Later that evening as they made their way home, the family stopped at a small restaurant. Suddenly, the little boy grabbed a cup and banged it on the table and said, "Momma, I want milk!" Within a short period of time, he could hear and speak, and soon was running and playing with other boys.

As news of the healing spread, questions and requests for healings grew daily. The Virgin responded in a very human way one day when, with a smile, she raised her hands, turned her eyes to heaven, and exclaimed: *God, help us all!*

In July, there was a startling addition to the apparitions. In answer to repeated pleas from the youth as to how they would be able to continue as visionaries, they were shown Jesus' head in a vision, clearly able to see His brown eyes, beard and long hair. The vision of Jesus was given to them, they were told, to prepare them for the suffering and persecution they had to endure as visionaries. The Blessed Virgin then told them: *My angels, I send you my Son, Jesus, who was tortured for His faith, and yet He endured everything. You also, my angels, will endure everything.*

She implored them to pray and have faith that they would survive this initial harassment and skepticism. How must we pray, they asked? *Continue to recite the Lord's Prayer, the Hail Mary, and the Glory Be* [in sequence] *seven times, but also add the Creed. Good-bye, my angels, go in the peace of God.*

Using this traditional prayer of the grandmothers of the region, the Virgin introduced the first lesson in prayer to her young seers. Later, she would ask for the rosary to be prayed daily; and, not just by Catholics, but by all people. Prayer, especially the rosary, would become the mainstay of all her messages.

It was soon evident that the lives of all involved would never be the same. This was the beginning of the final harvest of souls.

. . . . .

And he told them many things in parables, saying: "A sower went out to sow. And as he sowed, some seeds fell along the path, and the birds came and devoured them. Other seeds fell on rocky ground, where they had not much soil, and immediately they sprang up, since they had no depth of soil, but when the sun rose they were scorched; and since they had no root they withered away. Other seeds fell upon thorns, and the thorns grew up and choked them. Other seeds fell on good soil and brought forth grain, some a hundredfold, some sixty, some thirty. He who has ears, let him hear." Matthew 13: 3-9

Chapter 4

Good Soil

There was potential that Medjugorje might someday be good soil for spiritual conversion. Throughout the turmoil and struggle of generations, the villagers stubbornly clung to their Catholic faith. In 1933, as a visible sign of that faith, they had constructed a thirty-six-foot tall cement cross atop the mountain overlooking their fertile valley. The purpose was to mark the 1900th anniversary of the Cross. Mostly though, this undertaking reflected a mixture of faith and superstition in a common effort to obtain protection of the crops, the virtual life-blood of the people.

With the daily apparition now taking place in the village, questions were asked about the meaning of Cross mountain: "Had the cross been constructed as part of heaven's plan to bring the renewal of God to the people of the world through the apparitions?" Or, "Was this field for spiritual harvest chosen because of this act of faith by its people?" For believers, either thought would serve as an adequate answer.

For skeptics, however, interest was more pointed and demanding: "Why would heaven choose such an unlikely place to reveal incredible, supernatural messages to the world?" "Why would such awesome responsibility be placed in the hands of peasant children?" Such issues were stumbling blocks for the skeptics, but no obstacle at all for those who believed.

Medjugorje is small, rural and indistinguishable from hundreds of other villages scattered throughout a mountainous region—indistinguishable, that is, except for the huge cross atop the small mountain overlooking their valley. This fifteen-ton, concrete monolith accurately reflects the character and faith of the villagers. Legend has it that an actual relic of the original cross is embedded in its base. Years of harsh weather have aged, discolored, and chipped away chunks of cement from the edges of the cross. But its beauty and effect go beyond the exterior. The same can be said for the village and its people.

Most of western Hercegovina is poor and undeveloped, with little industry. The soil of the Brotnjo region, of which Medjugorje is part, is hard and stony. But once cleared, it is excellent, arable land for crop growing. After extremely hard manual labor, it becomes good soil providing high quality tobacco, splendid fruit trees, and fine vineyards that yield superior wines. Years of working the land form a lifestyle that hardens its residents, developing a resiliency that enables them to be self-sufficient.

For the people living in Medjugorje in June 1981, such resiliency was a must. It was also the root of a strong adherence to their Catholic faith. Under a Serb-dominated Marxist government, the practice of religion was grudgingly allowed; atheism was formally taught in the schools and children of religious families were ridiculed. Only those loyal to the Communist party line could hold important public jobs. Except for the most menial positions, livelihood for believers depended on the land and a handful of farm animals.

The young visionaries were representative of the villagers. Life for them was filled with daily chores and school. They were neither overly pious nor terribly bad. They were, as Mirjana herself would later describe, "neither good nor bad, just like everyone else." She went on to say, "When the apparitions began, my grandmother said: 'Why should the Madonna appear to the likes of you when you go around with boys?' I told her, well, she knows what we're like, and she doesn't want us to pretend to be something we're not!"

Yet, while ordinary in the sense of being part of the village, the children chosen to be visionaries were very different in temperament and personality. Prior to the apparitions, only three of them were close friends. Vicka, Ivanka and Mirjana were nearly inseparable and, while they knew the others, they had little in common with them other than school and the close proximity of their homes.

Suddenly finding themselves bound together as special witnesses of a supernatural event was both confusing and frightening. In the stress and harassment of the early days, a mini-struggle for leadership ensued, with Mirjana and Vicka dominating. In a short period, however, under the guidance of the Blessed Virgin, the visionaries developed into a close-knit unit with each having a distinct but informal role.

Mirjana was actually an outsider who, although having been born in Medjugorje, now lived and attended school in Sarajevo, coming to Medjugorje in the summers to stay with her grandparents. Bright and articulate, she was very much the typical teenager, her head filled with things of the world. By her own admission, she had paid little attention to spirituality and attended church more out of habit than desire. Personal prayer was rare for Mirjana. She hoped for a career in agronomy after attending the university in Sarajevo.

Pretty, blond, and outgoing, Mirjana became a natural leader and spokesperson for the visionaries. At times, it was thought by some that she went too far, adding personal interpretation to parts of the Madonna's messages. Coming from the city as she did, Mirjana was the main target for accusations. Rumors circulated that she might have brought drugs to the village and convinced the others to try them; thus, the visions might be nothing more than the hallucinatory effect of drugs. Such rumors died down in the following days with the consistency of the visionaries' stories.

Mirjana's good friend Ivanka was the first to see the Virgin and was amazed to be included as a visionary. She, too, was typical in her teenage ways. A very attractive, dark-haired girl, Ivanka was sure of her path in life. She wanted to marry as quickly as possible and settle in the village to raise her family as part of a lifestyle that had changed little over the centuries.

But Ivanka had just lost her mother and was in a state of grief and depression at the time the apparitions began. Naturally, skeptics assumed that since she was the first to see the Blessed Virgin, she was desperately trying to replace the loss of her mother by claiming to see the Virgin. That theory might have had credibility if the apparitions had lasted only a few days, but with the passing weeks, it became clear that a young girl's grief could not explain the strength with which Ivanka stuck to her story, even in the midst of ongoing and strenuous harassment. Her joy came in the moments of the daily appearance of the Virgin. It was more than enough to sustain her.

Marija, quiet and good-natured, may have assumed the role of visionary intended for her thirteen-year-old sister Milka who had been one of the group to see the vision on the first day. When the others came running to Milka's home the following day, claiming that the apparition was occurring again, she was working in the fields on orders from her mother who did not believe her daughter's claim of having seen the Virgin. Instead, Marija and little Jakov, who was visiting with Marija at the time, returned with the others to the apparition site, thus completing the contingent of youths who would become daily visionaries.

After Marija had experienced the apparition, her mother was convinced that Milka had truly seen the Madonna on the first day as she claimed. Marija insisted her sister accompany her the next day and stand right behind her. Milka did, but sadly, she was unable to see the vision.

Marija is gifted with an ability to make everyone around her comfortable and at ease. Unobtrusive and humble, she had planned to become a beautician, but after several weeks of the apparitions, she stated she wanted to enter a convent, adding that before the apparitions, God was distant; now, she wanted to give the rest of her life to serving Him.

Cheerful, outgoing, and with a radiant, seemingly perpetual smile, Vicka easily became the "ambassador" of the apparitions. Prior to that fateful day when the Blessed Virgin first appeared, Vicka's family was known for having a strong faith. One priest stated with some amusement that her family could be heard most evenings by their neighbors loudly reciting prayers. Another priest, who had taught Vicka her catechism, described her as incapable of telling a lie.

This vibrant young girl seemed to have no fear of authority, answering priest and pilgrim alike concerning mundane questions about the apparitions. Once, when a priest made a query about a particular message, and then asked after she had answered, "Are you sure?" Vicka laughed and said, "Of course I'm sure—I was there!" Another time when local authorities had taken the children to police headquarters for questioning, a policeman had threatened Vicka, putting a gun to her temple in an attempt to intimidate her. Testily, she gave a short laugh and said, "Why would you waste a bullet on the likes of me when the economy is so bad?"

Ivan was almost the direct opposite of Vicka. Shy, serious, and introverted, he was visibly uncomfortable around pilgrims and the media and did not enjoy the notoriety of being a visionary. But he was in a constant state of awe that the Virgin had chosen him. He later explained that when he first saw the image of the Virgin on the hillside, he ran away out of fear that he had never really acknowledged God as a part of his life. Ivan immediately went to his room, locked the door and began to pray. His mother was stunned, and would later state that she believed her son was actually seeing the Blessed Virgin when she found a rosary in his jean pocket as she was doing the laundry.

Two months later, Ivan would enter a seminary with the intention of becoming a priest, an attempt that would fail academically and personally. But the desire and effort indicated just how deeply he was spiritually moved with the realization that the Madonna was appearing daily to him and the others at Medjugorje.

The question on the minds of many villagers was what was ten-year-old Jakov doing among the selected visionaries? A clever, impish, strong-headed boy, so like other young boys his age, Jakov Colo was hardly what you would expect to play an integral part in such a miracle. His interests were far from prayer and church attendance; closer to the mark was an interest in sports, especially soccer. Even after his inclusion as a visionary, he was not above once asking the Madonna to tell him the score of an upcoming championship soccer match, which included one of his favorite teams! The Virgin merely smiled.

Jakov's father was rarely present in their small hovel of a home, constantly away working as a migrant worker in Austria, leaving the task of raising and providing for his only son to his wife. Thus, the little boy immersed himself in games as an escape from the harsh realities of daily life. But once the visions became a regular part of each day, Jakov was always in attendance at the evening Mass. He spoke with awe about the Virgin; her daily appearance became the most important part of his life, and he spoke with seriousness and pointed politeness when interviewed by media and priests.

These were the young people raised to instant notoriety as visionaries of a unique, supernatural phenomenon that would transform them and their village forever. The transformation would be spiritual; individual personalities would remain the same. The same could be said of their village which became, as it were, new holy ground without ever losing its own special character. For both the children and the village, the essence of what had always been, remained.

As the Virgin continued to appear, the visionaries moved beyond the mere transmission of her messages; they became living examples of them as well. Each assumed a specific role with greater responsibility given in the early months to Mirjana, Vicka, and Marija.

Mirjana seemed to have received a deeper understanding about the state of the church. Her good friend Vicka became the dominant mystic, with the responsibility of revealing the fate of the world as given through the messages. Marija was chosen to give particular messages to pilgrims and priests. Later, she would be the one to receive and communicate the Virgin's messages meant for the general public. Each was also given responsibility to pray for specific intentions: Mirjana for unbelievers, Vicka and Jakov for the sick and handicapped, Marija for souls in purgatory, Ivan for youth, and Ivanka for families.

Thus, Medjugorje, a humble place, a place of little things and unchanging daily life, became a new Bethlehem where the world would once again discover the presence of God. Six young people, ordinary in every sense by outward appearances, become relaters of heavenly messages meant for the entire world. It all seemed so unlikely. Yet, the modus operandi is ageless: God chooses poverty, simplicity, and the ordinary in order to manifest Himself.

There were those who continued to question the reason for this place and these children. For believers, the answer was clear almost from the first day: the abundant fruit of lives transformed as a deep, spiritual peace settled over the village.

But for the unbeliever, no explanation would suffice.

.   .   .   .   .

At that time Jesus declared, "I thank thee, Father, Lord of heaven and earth, that thou hast hidden these things from the wise and understanding and revealed them to babes . . ."

Matthew 11:25

Chapter 5

Taking Root

The apparitions continued into September 1981, much to the delight of the visionaries and the village. Having no previous knowledge of past apparitions, the visionaries were told about Lourdes, France, where the Blessed Virgin had appeared a total of eighteen times in 1858. They naturally assumed that she would appear at Medjugorje the same number of times. Once the eighteenth daily apparition had come and gone, they asked her how much longer she was going to appear. She smiled, paused, and then said: *Is it, after all, that I am boring you?* She later added when asked the same question, *As long as you wish, my angels!*

Was it possible, the visionaries wondered, that she would continue coming every day? The news spread rapidly throughout the region and soon even larger crowds were coming to Medjugorje. The surge created heavy overloads on utilities, pushing reserves to the maximum. Daily work was disrupted, and roads were jammed resulting in formerly unheard of traffic snarls. In addition, the Franciscan priests of the parish were unsure just what to do with so many people seeking spiritual guidance and answers to questions about the apparitions.

Because of the rapidly growing crowds, the local Communist authorities were fearful that insurrection was about to take place. They continued their merciless harassment of the visionaries, threatening them and members of their families. Without notice, they would pick them up and transport them to police headquarters in nearby Citluk for long hours of questioning. Family members were threatened with the loss of jobs and arrest if the nonsense did not cease. Pilgrims coming to the area were stopped, searched, and delayed for hours.

The harshest threats were saved for Franciscan priest Jozo Zovko, pastor of St. James Church—by this time a strong supporter and spiritual director for the children; and, for the bishop

22

of the diocese, Pavao Zanic. Government officials made it clear to both that they wanted the daily gatherings stopped immediately. The blunt alternative was jail.

In the beginning, Father Jozo, who had been pastor in Medjugorje only six months prior to the start of the apparitions, severely questioned the young visionaries. He could not understand why people were not coming to the church for Mass and confession if these visions were really from God. Several weeks after they had begun, the villagers were still flocking to the hill every evening. He sat alone in his church one evening in deep prayer, asking God for a sign if what was happening was indeed from Him. Suddenly, he heard a distinct male voice say: "First, go out and protect the children!"

Startled, Father Jozo looked around the church. The message was repeated. A banging on the church door interrupted his encounter and when he opened the door, the visionaries came tumbling in, pleading for him to protect them as the police were chasing them. The pastor quickly whisked them to the rectory and placed them in a small room before returning to the front of the building determined to protect them. Within minutes the police came and brusquely asked Father Jozo if he had seen the children. He told them he had, but inexplicably, they did not wait to hear more. Instead, they ran off in another direction.

Father Jozo and the children returned to the church. A short time later, the Virgin appeared in apparition and the priest who had doubted was suddenly *able to see her* just as the children did! From that moment, Father Jozo became their staunchest supporter and defender, a role that would soon cost him his freedom.

In October, the authorities made good on their threat. Father Jozo was arrested and charged with fostering insurrection through a highly charged sermon he delivered shortly after he had witnessed ·the Virgin in apparition. The authorities deemed the homily as a direct attack on the Marxist system of government. It was just the excuse needed to arrest the priest and thus, hopefully, bring the apparitions to an end.

As for Bishop Zanic, in the four-month period of harassment by local Communist authorities, he completely changed his attitude towards the apparitions. His initially zealous support turned to bitter opposition. So interested was he in the beginning weeks, he had made five visits to the parish to see and talk with the visionaries and the priests. In a homily in July, the bishop had even proclaimed his belief for all the world to hear: "Six simple children like these would have told all in half an hour, if anybody had been manipulating them. I assure you that none of the priests have done any such thing . . . furthermore, I am convinced the children are not lying . . ."

What could have happened to cause the bishop to change his mind so radically? Simply put, the escalation of a petty squabble between Franciscan and secular priests[4] lay at the root of the bishop's about-face. The bishop himself was not a Franciscan, and therein lay the problem. The Franciscans had been in the diocese for centuries, serving the people through the worst times of invasion and war, so much so that they were affectionately referred to as "uncles" by the faithful.

In September 1980, the year before the apparitions started, the newly named bishop of Mostar immediately began shifting parishes in his diocese from Franciscan to secular authority. The Franciscans were outraged, as were the people of the parishes in question. It was the parishioners who vigorously insisted that Franciscan priests assigned to the parishes in question continue to serve, which they did.

When Bishop Zanic learned of this, he retaliated by making an example of two of the most popular young Franciscans, initiating action to have them expelled from their order—and from the priesthood. Holy war broke out. The situation could have and should have been handled quietly within the diocese. But true to the heritage of the region, it became a crux of public confrontation and was unofficially dubbed the "Hercegovina Case."

Worsening the situation, the visionaries were persuaded by a Franciscan priest to ask the Blessed Virgin to comment on the problem. Surprisingly, she did. According to the visionaries, she stated that the bishop had been "misled and misinformed," and

---

4, Secular priests have no affiliation with a specific order such as the Franciscans or Jesuits. Most priests in the Catholic Church are secular priests.

"should reconsider" his banning of the two Franciscans. That did it. When Bishop Zanic heard this message delivered to him in fervent terms personally by visionary Vicka, he exclaimed, "The Blessed Mother of God would never speak to a bishop that way!"

From that moment on, Bishop Zanic became a staunch opponent of the apparitions.

Word among the Franciscans, however, was that the bishop had been looking for a reason to distance himself from the apparitions, fearing he, too, would be jailed by the Communist authorities. This latest turn in the confrontation with the Franciscans proved to be a perfect way out.

. . . . .

The bishop's stunning and sudden rejection was distressing, even more so coupled with Father's Jozo's conviction to three years in jail. The pastor of St. James would eventually serve eighteen months at hard labor. However, the Blessed Virgin implored the people through the visionaries to listen to her messages and begin enacting her requests for prayer, fasting, penance, and frequent confession. If heaven's plan through the apparitions were to succeed, the Church would have to be intricately involved; there was no other way. That was the order of life in the village and in the region.

Things were soon put back on the right track, ironically by orders from the government to move the apparitions from the hillside. There were to be no more outside demonstrations, that is, apparitions, which the authorities still viewed as the beginnings of insurrection. If the young people and the villagers insisted on continuing these gatherings, they must move them into the church. Thus, the apparitions were soon occurring each evening in a small side chapel on the right side of the altar of Saint James Church. Huge crowds now filled the church and its surrounding grounds. The formation of a daily spiritual regimen was soon implemented. It would become the foundation of conversion for millions throughout the world. Unbeknownst to the authorities, their harassment accomplished exactly what the Virgin desired of the people!

As envisioned by Sister Briege McKenna when she had prayed over Father Tomislav Vlasic at the Rome charismatic conference, the "living spiritual waters" were flowing freely in Medjugorje. Father Tomislav was now the pastor at Saint James, taking the place of imprisoned Father Jozo. Overflowing crowds gathered early every evening, filling the church and the surrounding grounds while the rosary was said in preparation for Gospa's appearance. Upon her arrival, a powerful silence descended on the gathering; at her departure, the rosary was completed and the Mass began. Following Mass, the people would say the glorious mysteries of the rosary, and then close the evening with the Virgin's original prayer request.

Even though many throughout the region paid little attention to the messages of the apparitions, the villagers of Medjugorje showed definite signs of changing attitudes and habits. They were attending evening Mass regularly; few were working in the evenings or on Sunday. There were noticeable differences in how they treated each other, too, as the infamy of family feuds that had been a trademark of the community began to fade.

These important changes had begun in the early weeks of the apparitions. Father Jozo, once convinced the apparitions were from God, knew that without acceptance of the messages in thought, word, and deed, the purpose of the supernatural grace would fail. The people of Medjugorje and the surrounding region had to become the example for those who would come in the future from around the world.

Shortly after undergoing his own transformation from skeptic to believer, the pastor of Saint James called an evening meeting in the church. Once congregated, the villagers were astounded to hear Father Jozo tell them of his own experience in seeing the Virgin. But that was not all. The people of Medjugorje, he concluded, must become an example for others; no one was leaving the church until they forgave each other. He then folded his arms and waited.

There was uneasy shifting and a low, continuous murmur. Finally a burly villager stood up, red-faced and nervous. He walked over to another man with whom he had feuded for years, and stuck out his hand. The man stood up and instead of taking his hand, embraced him, a rare act especially between Croatian men so hardened by daily toil and years of oppression. In seconds, the church was in happy bedlam as mass forgiveness began the conversion process for the people of Medjugorje.

The wave of conversions continued to gather momentum. With each apparition, questions were asked, and the Virgin gave answers. Now, the people were anxiously awaiting each message. It was soon evident that every message and answer was simply confirmation of what was recorded in the Bible, both Old and New Testaments. The focus was always on God.

Questions regarding the trials of daily life dominated, as in the case of one woman who wanted to leave her husband because he was cruel to her. The Virgin Mary answered: *Let her remain close to him and accept her suffering. Jesus, Himself, also suffered.* The answer was startling in a world that had come to accept divorce as casually as changing jobs.

But curiosity still prevailed. People wanted to know mundane details about things of the world. Were "flying saucers" real? Would there be a third world war? After one session with such questions, the Blessed Virgin told two of the visionaries: *Don't ask useless questions dictated by curiosity. The most important thing is to pray, my angels.*

There were also constant questions concerning faiths: Why are there so many different faiths? Are all religions the same? In a region simmering with hate for those of divergent religious beliefs, the answers were startlingly direct and profound: *Members of all faiths are equal before God . . . God rules over each faith just like a sovereign rules over his kingdom . . . In the world, all religions are not the same because all people have not complied with the commandments of God. They reject and disparage them.*

The Blessed Virgin's responses were immediately seized upon and used as evidence by skeptics of the apparitions, as well as leaders of the regional religious factions. She had made all religions the same, they exclaimed. But the visionaries quickly corrected the misconceptions after presenting them to the Blessed Virgin. She was saying that all people of all faiths were equal before God, not all faiths—an important difference! What the Virgin was really getting at was how can anyone live the messages if they do not respect all people regardless of their beliefs?

The antagonists pressed on: Is she telling us that all churches are the same and accepted equally by God? Her answer: *In some, the strength of prayer to God is greater, in others, smaller. That depends on the priests who motivate others to pray. It depends also on the power which they have.*

At the further prodding of priests and theologians, the visionaries asked the Blessed Virgin if she is the Mother of God and if she went to heaven before or after her death. Again, she answered directly: I am the Mother of God and the Queen of Peace. I went to heaven before death. And another sticky point of debate between faiths: Are there other intermediaries besides Jesus between God and man? There is only one mediator between God and man, and it is Jesus Christ.

It was an incredible period for the visionaries, their families, the villagers, and the authorities of the Church. So much information! Could this really be from heaven? Even with all that had occurred, many priests did not think so. Meanwhile, Serb-dominated civil authorities remained convinced this was simply a Croatian ploy leading to full insurrection against the government.

It was the best and worst of times for all involved.

· · · · ·

"And it shall come to pass afterward, that I will pour out my spirit on all flesh; your sons and your daughters shall prophesy, your old men shall dream dreams, and your young men shall see visions. Even upon the menservants and the maidservants in those days, I will pour out my spirit. And I will give portents in the heavens and on the earth, blood, fire, and columns of smoke."

Joel 2:28-30

Chapter 6

Early Growth

As if it were not enough to appear in daily apparition and deliver profound teachings through her messages, the Blessed Virgin provided numerous supernatural signs in and around Medjugorje. Many villagers and visiting pilgrims witnessed these miraculous events. These little *"gifts"* were given, according to the Virgin, to *"reawaken people's faith."*

One of the earliest of these signs involved the visionaries themselves on the first day of conversation with the Blessed Virgin. When she appeared that day, the children ran up the side of the hill to where she was at a rate of speed far exceeding normal physical ability. Vicka was barefoot, yet the sharp-edged stones along the pathway did not cut her feet. Young Jakov knelt on a thorn-covered bush and the others were sure he would be terribly hurt. Afterwards, he was found to be unharmed.

Many of the villagers and, later, others who came from throughout the region, would occasionally be able to see the three bursts of light that always preceded the Virgin's daily appearance. On the third day of the apparitions, this light covered not only the spot on the hill where she appeared, but also the village and the entire region. It was seen by thousands of people.

Another amazing sign concerning this supernatural light occurred as the apparitions continued into a seventh day. The Communist authorities, in an attempt to stop the apparitions, devised a plan to remove the visionaries from the normal apparition site. Two social workers from Citluk were sent by local officials to persuade the visionaries to go for a ride with them through the surrounding area. Since the visionaries knew the officials personally, they agreed to go. The hidden motive was to keep the young people away from the hill past the usual time of the Virgin's appearance, so there would be no apparition.

As the time approached, the visionaries realized what was happening. They became upset and threatened to jump from the moving vehicle. Alarmed, the social workers stopped the car; then, along with the visionaries, they observed a light illuminating the distant hillside of the apparitions. The light suddenly began moving toward them until it finally settled over the visionaries as they knelt in ecstasy on the side of the road for their daily encounter with the Virgin.

Twenty days after the apparitions began, thousands saw a remarkable sign in the sky. In sharp cloud formation, the Croatian word for peace, mir, appeared and stayed for a long period of time, hovering over the large cement cross on Krizevac Mountain. This and other phenomena involved the rugged cross that overlooked the valley. The Blessed Virgin told the visionaries that she prayed to her Son early each morning at the foot of this cross. Several times the cross totally disappeared from view for a short period. It would then reappear, sometimes spinning or rotating on its axis.[5]

Even with all this, the greatest and most commonly seen sign at Medjugorje has become known as the "miracle of the sun." This phenomenon first occurred during the final apparition of the Blessed Virgin Mary in Fatima, Portugal, on October 13, 1917 (more on this apparition later). A crowd in excess of 70,000 people were witnesses that day, many of them reporting that the sun suddenly began spinning, moving about, and throwing off the colors of the rainbow. It then began to dance around, swooping down close to the panicking people. Later, a variety of religious images formed around it. It was a stunning, unbelievable display that had many of the witnesses thinking the end of the world was upon them.

Possibly, that was the objective. Here is the most stable, heavenly body in the sky, provider and symbol of all life, suddenly abandoning the laws of physics. It was impossible; believer and unbeliever alike were left without explanation. For the "Woman

---

5. I personally witnessed this phenomenon in May 1986 during my first pilgrimage to Medjugorje. The cross disappeared as we boarded our bus for departure to Dubrovnik. Ten minutes later, as we were driving from the area, it reappeared and began spinning on its axis.

clothed with the sun" (Revelation 12:1), it was the perfect sign to tell humanity that God indeed was speaking directly to them through her supernatural appearances.

The miracle of the sun was first witnessed in Medjugorje on August 2, 1981. Approximately 150 people saw it while on Podbrdo Hill, the place where the Virgin had first appeared. Just as the sun was about to set, it suddenly seemed to come toward them and then to recede and begin spinning on its axis. People were able to look directly at the sun without injury to their eyes. At the end, a large white cloud came upon the hillside and settled over the sun which then returned to its normal state. The entire phenomenon lasted approximately fifteen minutes.

For the visionaries and followers of Medjugorje, it was no coincidence that this sign of the sun first occurred on August 2, the Feast of Our Lady, Queen of the Angels. Many of the people witnessing the miracle on this day reported seeing large globules of different colored light moving around the sun. They also reported seeing images of the Blessed Virgin and a great number of angels with trumpets coming out of the sun. Then, according to some, a large heart appeared with six small hearts under it, clearly a representation of the Madonna and her six young visionaries.

Near the end of the first year of apparitions, many people saw the huge cement cross on the top of Krizevac Mountain transform itself into a brilliant, shimmering light and then into a silhouette of the Blessed Virgin Mary. The visionaries were asked to have the Virgin explain this and the other phenomena: *All of these signs are designed to strengthen your faith until I leave you the visible and permanent sign.*

The visionaries were questioned about this "permanent sign." They explained that the Virgin had said the permanent sign would be the greatest of the phenomena of supernatural signs in Medjugorje. They added that they had been shown this sign in the course of the apparitions (by way of an inner vision). It will be left permanently on the hill at the very spot where the first apparition took place. The sign will be visible to everyone and will be proof that these apparitions are indeed from God. It will be able to be photographed, televised and seen—but not touched. When questioned about it not being able to be touched, the visionaries were not clear if this meant it would be forbidden to touch it, or that it would be impossible to touch it because of its composition.

As to when the permanent sign will occur, the date is known only to the visionaries who say that it is one of three warnings, which are actually the first three secrets that will be given to the world shortly after the apparitions cease occurring daily. There is no set date or indication of just how soon the warnings will occur once the apparitions are over.

The Virgin later added this about the permanent sign: *The sign will come, but you must not spend too much time looking for it. My urgent message to you is, be converted! Pass this message to all my children wherever they are. There is no trouble I will not take, no suffering I will not bear to save them. I shall beg my Son not to punish the world, but I implore you, be converted, change your lives. You cannot begin to imagine what lies ahead . . . so, I beg you again, be converted!*

Again, she stresses the importance of living the messages in daily life. What would any of us do, if we knew the exact date the permanent sign would be given? Or what the future chastisements might be? Would we not pray, fast and do penance as she urges us constantly with every appearance?

While the permanent sign will be the greatest of the supernatural phenomena in Medjugorje, one of the most common and prolific signs has been the color change from silver to gold of the metal links of pilgrims' rosaries. This sometimes occurs while the rosaries are being used in prayer. Old rosaries change just as frequently as new ones, and occasionally the process is reversed, with gold changing to silver. Some skeptics, wanting to take their investigation to a higher scientific level, brought these altered rosaries to qualified jewelers for testing. They were shocked to discover that in some cases the coating on the metal is actually gold!

Another startling sign took place after an apparition at Jakov's home in late October. The letters "MIR LJUDIMA" (Peace to the people) appeared in brilliant gold on one of the walls in his house. This phenomenon underlined again the Blessed Virgin's call for the people to reconcile with one another. She continued, sometimes gently and other times with extreme gravity, to warn them to seek peace through prayer.

Such was the case shortly after the sign had appeared on the wall. The visionaries were praying when, suddenly, the Virgin intervened: *Oh my Son Jesus, forgive these sins; there are so many of them!* They paused and became silent, and she added, *Continue to pray, because prayer is the salvation of the people.*

Regardless of the many signs and wonders accompanying the daily appearances of the Blessed Virgin Mary in Medjugorje, strong skeptics remained, including many priests. Ivan asked Gospa how to help doubting priests understand the apparitions. She answered directly: *It is necessary to tell them that from the very beginning I have been conveying the message of God to the world. It is a great pity not to believe in it. Faith is a vital element, but one cannot compel a person to believe. Faith is the foundation from which everything flows.*

. . . . .

. . . [H]ow shall we escape if we neglect such a great salvation? It was declared at first by the Lord, and it was attested to us by those who heard him, while God also bore witness by signs and wonders and various miracles and by gifts of the Holy Spirit distributed according to his own will. Hebrews 2:3-4

Chapter 7

Storm Warning

There was another important "sign" given on the first day of the apparitions. This sign, an ominous one, did not come through the intercession of the Blessed Virgin Mary, but from the one who is always at work counteracting her mission.

This forbidding sign came suddenly in the early morning hours of June 24, 1981, as a full-fury summer storm enveloped the valley in minutes, turning the calm of night into unholy terror. Many villagers, startled out of deep sleep by ear-splitting peals of thunder and continuous streaks of lightning, were certain doomsday had arrived. Torrents of hard rain were driven sideways by furious gusts of wind; lightning struck the post office setting it afire. Claps of thunder caused the ground to tremble as though moved by an earthquake. The storm subsided as quickly as it had come, leaving the villagers shaken as they fought the raging fire at the post office.

Only later would these sudden minutes of dark fury be seen as the portentous calling card of the Prince of Darkness, coming to do battle again with the Woman sent by heaven. Approximately sixteen hours later, in the calm of day, Ivanka first saw the Blessed Virgin on the hillside. Another battle in the age-old clash between good and evil had begun; the new battlefield was the village of Medjugorje.

Two months later, on August 2, the same day the miracle of the sun was first witnessed in Medjugorje, a strange event took place late in the evening. After the Mass, a small group of villagers gathered with the visionaries in an isolated field away from the church to sing and pray in honor of the feast day (Our Lady of the Angels, as mentioned in the preceding chapter). The Virgin suddenly appeared without notice to the visionaries. Marija startled the gathering when she announced, "Our Lady says she will allow those who so desire to come and touch her."

34

As the people rushed forward to "touch" the Virgin, the vision-aries would tell them: "You are touching her veil . . . now you are touching her head . . . her dress." Suddenly Marija shouted: "Oh! Our Lady is disappearing and she is completely blackened!"

Marija's neighbor, Marinko Ivankovic, a stalwart defender and protector of the children from the first days of the apparitions, asked Marija what had happened. "Oh, Marinko," she replied, "there were sinners here and as they touched her, her dress got darker and darker until it turned black." Marija then asked that all present go to confession the following day.

Appalled by this visible evidence of the power of sin, Marinko loudly echoed Marija's call for confession, making sure all were aware of it. He then learned in further conversation with Marija that another unusual and unannounced apparition had occurred earlier that evening. As Marija was changing into jeans before coming to the field, the Virgin suddenly appeared to her in her room, telling her: *The devil is trying to infiltrate himself here in order to get something. My Son wants to win over all the souls, but the devil is exerting himself to get something. He is making every effort and wants at any price to infiltrate among you.*

"I am not sure if Marija understood Our Lady correctly or not," Marinko was later quoted, "but she stated that Our Lady also said that she does not know how all of this will turn out—if the devil will succeed or not . . ."

What was the exact meaning of the Blessed Virgin's warning? Was it about the devil wanting to infiltrate among the visionaries, or Medjugorje as a whole? It is not clear, but there was little doubt from her unusual added apparitions to Marija on this special feast day, or from her words, that the battle was on. Without the peo-ple's response to her pleadings for prayer, fasting, and penance, the outcome remained unclear. Response could only come by a free will choosing of good over evil.

The next day, there were long lines in and around the church for confession, and more the following day. Priests who heard the confessions were astounded at the number and intensity. Pleased with the response, the Virgin urged the people through the vision-aries to continue on a path of repentance and conversion.

Shortly thereafter, the visionaries disclosed to the priests that the Madonna was giving them information concerning the future. According to them, she would progressively reveal to each of them ten future events that would occur in the world. They were not to divulge these events, or *secrets*, as they were called, to anyone until given permission by the Virgin. Not even to the Franciscans or their own family members. Once a visionary had received all ten secrets, the Virgin would no longer appear on a daily basis to that particular visionary.

The only detail concerning the secrets revealed at the time was that the permanent sign was the third of three warnings (the warnings are actually the first three secrets) that would be given shortly after the apparitions ceased with the last visionary. Later, Mirjana would add this about the permanent sign: "When the permanent sign appears, unbelievers will run to the hill and pray for forgiveness . . ."

While the Virgin emphasized that attention to the ten secrets should be minimal—that is, know about them, but focus primarily on her messages, which lead to daily conversion—one can assume some details based on various statements by the visionaries. As stated, the first three secrets are warnings given to the world to prove that the apparitions are truly from God. The next three seem to concern the village of Medjugorje and the visionaries personally, with perhaps different secrets for the individual visionaries. The last four secrets are clearly about chastisements that will occur in the world.[6]

Reassurance was given later when the Virgin said that because of the prayers, fasting, and penance by those responding to her call, the seventh secret, or chastisement, had been mitigated. Other chastisements can also be mitigated, she revealed through Mirjana, but the tenth will occur, because "everyone will not convert."

Mirjana later revealed that Satan had appeared to her during this time to try and sway her away from the Blessed Virgin Mary. She related that one evening, as she prepared for her daily apparition, there was suddenly a flash of light and he appeared. She

---

6. This outline is strictly a personal opinion of the author, based on early statements given by the visionaries.

described him as "horrible and black all over, terrifying." After passing out momentarily, Mirjana awakened, she relates, to "find him standing there, laughing . . . he told me I would be very beautiful and very happy in love and life, and so on, but that I would have no need of the Madonna or of my faith . . . Then something inside of me shouted, No! I began to shake and to feel sick, and then he disappeared and the Madonna came, telling me that it would not happen again . . ."

Later, the Blessed Virgin would add this message: *The Devil tries to impose his power on you, but you must remain strong and persevere in your faith. You must pray and fast. I will always be close to you.*

The visionaries, the villagers, and the Church would need that reassurance. The storm warning was over, but the battle was just beginning.

. . . . .

I will put enmity between you and the woman, and between your seed and her seed; he shall bruise your head, and you shall bruise his heel.   Genesis 3:15

PART II

Planting

First of all you must understand this, that scoffers will come in the last days with scoffing, following their own passions and saying, "Where is the promise of His coming? For ever since the fathers fell asleep, all things have continued as they were from the beginning of creation." . . . But do not ignore this one fact, beloved . . . The Lord is not slow about His promise as some count slowness, but is forbearing toward you, not wishing that any should perish, but that all should reach repentance. But the day of the Lord will come like a thief.

2 Peter: 3:3-4, 8-10

Chapter 8

The Seeds of La Salette and Fatima

What was happening in Medjugorje was not too different from apparitions of the Blessed Virgin Mary in past times of trouble. Such occurrences dot the pages of history. Many theologians acknowledge the Virgin's activity in the past two centuries as that of a special messenger sent in times of extreme crisis to warn and give guidance directly from heaven. In this sense, the Virgin's activities continue a precedent set in the pages of the Old Testament where we see God periodically raising up prophets for the people in times of urgent necessity. The modern era is no different.

As far back as 1531, the Lady sent from heaven came several times to a recently converted Christian Indian named Juan Diego in an area of Mexico called Guadalupe. From that series of apparitions, more than seven million pagans were converted to Christianity. Ironically, as these new converts built up the Church in what would become the nation of Mexico, seven million European Catholics were deserting the Church to form a multiplicity of Christian denominations with new theologies. That same year, 1531, is often used to mark the beginning of the Protestant Reformation movement in the region that would eventually form the country of Germany.

In 1830, the Blessed Virgin Mary appeared to a young nun named Catherine Laboure at a convent in Paris located on a street called the Rue du Bac. Again, it was a time of civil disruption in the region. The shock waves of the reign of terror that had followed the French Revolution were still being felt in direct attacks against the authority of the Church and her members. During the apparitions, the Virgin requested that a special medal be cast. In a vision, she showed Catherine both the front and back of the medal. No sooner had it been made than miracles started happening in abundance. The "Miraculous Medal" of Rue du Bac spread swiftly across the country and the region. Today, it is still the most popular medal of modern times.

Later, in 1858, the Virgin appeared eighteen times to Bernadette Soubirous, a young, poor and sick girl, in a dirty grotto close to Lourdes, France. During one of the apparitions, the Blessed Virgin asked Bernadette to wash her face in the fountain—but there was no fountain, so Bernadette dug a hole in the ground and with the muddy water, began to wipe her face, much to the mocking amusement of onlookers. A short time later, however, a spring came up from that spot, the now-famous fountain of water that has healing attributes. Millions come to Lourdes annually to bath in this water and pray for a cure. More than sixty-four such cures have been recognized after exhaustive study. Lourdes remains one of the world's greatest fountains of conversion and a place of extraordinary peace and prayer.

There were more apparitions during the final years of the last century, especially in France, but that which occurred in Knock, Ireland, is of particular importance. It's prophetic and, one could say, apocalyptic nature, is striking.

The apparition took place in 1879, in the evening, during a driving rain storm. Two women from the small village of Knock were walking near the local church when they noticed luminous figures at the gable end. They immediately identified one of the figures as the Blessed Virgin; the others were Saint Joseph and Saint John the Evangelist, the beloved disciple of Jesus, who was seen holding a book of Scripture. As darkness fell, other people joined the witnesses and soon there was a crowd. All of them could see an altar with a young lamb on it in front of a cross; one boy saw angels over the altar. There were no sounds and no messages. The Blessed Virgin Mary looked with adoration at the lamb, as did the two other figures. The symbolism of the lamb, cross and altar has been understood as a symbolic reference to the sacrificial death of Jesus, with Mary in front representing her role as mediator. For me, this apparition is the most ecumenical in history in that the figures silently adore the Lamb who, of course, represents Jesus.

While all apparitions are related in purpose, the strongest link between Medjugorje and the Blessed Virgin's previous visits begins in 1846 with a powerful message given during a single-appearance vision in La Salette, France. This apparition, in my opinion, marks the beginning of a special Marian time period. It is closely linked in content and urgency to the apparition of Fatima, Portugal, in 1917. Together, La Salette and Fatima relate directly to the apparitions of Medjugorje and, therefore, merit careful consideration.

The village of La Salette, located in the Alps, was one of a skimpily populated collection of hamlets, not unlike the region around Medjugorje. But unlike Medjugorje, the Blessed Virgin came only one time to this village, on Saturday, September 19, 1846, to two young children who were serving as shepherds hired by local ranchers. Melanie Calvet, 14, and Maximin Giraud, 11, were checking on the cattle when suddenly they saw a large circle of brilliant light in the ravine below. Running towards it, they watched as it began to open, revealing the figure of a woman surrounded by light. She was seated with her face in her hands, crying. As they moved nearer, she arose, opened her arms, and began speaking to them in perfect French: *Come to me my children, do not be afraid; I am here to tell you something of great importance.*

The children looked at each other puzzled since they did not clearly understand her words. The woman in the light then changed to their local dialect and repeated the greeting. After identifying herself, she gave Maximin a secret message. She then turned to Melanie and gave a long message, to be kept secret until 1858. Parts of that message are as follows: *The priests, my Son's ministers, by their bad lives, their irreverence and impiety in celebrating the Sacred Mysteries, by love of money, love of honor and pleasures, the priests have become cesspools of impurity . . . The heads, the leaders of the people of God have neglected prayer and penance, and the devil has darkened their intelligence . . . Bad books will abound upon the earth, the spirits of darkness will propagate a universal falling off everywhere in all that concerns the service of God. They will have great power over nature. There will be churches where the spirits are served . . .*

The Blessed Virgin then turned her attention to the world in general: *God is going to strike in an unprecedented manner. Woe to the inhabitants of the earth! There will be a general war which will be dreadful* [World War I] . . . *Nature cries out for vengeance upon mankind and groans in terror in apprehension of what must come upon the earth, so sullied with crimes* . . . *Before this happens there will be a sort of false peace in the world. People will think only of amusing themselves. The wicked will lend themselves to all sorts of sins* . . .

The message ends with an urgent call to return to God: *I address an urgent appeal to the earth: I summon the true disciples of God who lives and reigns in heaven. I summon the true imitators of Christ the God-Man* . . .

Reaction to the message of La Salette at that time was the same as it is today with Medjugorje: for the most part, disbelief and lack of interest by clergy and laity alike. Yet, both these incredible, heavenly interventions have the same purpose: to lead mankind back to God.

Nearly seventy years after La Salette, on May 13, 1917, the Blessed Virgin came for the people of the twentieth century, appearing in the little village of Fatima, Portugal. Once more, her visit took place at a moment of grave crisis. World War I was threatening to bring an end to civilization, just as the Virgin had predicted at La Salette. The world was shaken by a period of tremendous religious, social, and political upheaval. Russia was in chaos. And in Portugal, the Christian faith was challenged to the point of extinction by a Marxist-leaning government.

Into this setting came the Mother of Jesus—again. And again, she came to peasant children, this time, three of them: Lucia, a devout girl of ten, and her cousins Francisco, age nine, and little seven-year-old Jacinta. Similarly to La Salette, the children were tending sheep in the hills when the Virgin first appeared on the thirteenth day of May 1917; she would appear to them on the thirteenth of the month for the next five months with the final apparition in October.

During the course of the Fatima apparitions, the children were given messages, taught to pray, and, much to their surprise, shown vivid scenes of hell (the vision of hell is actually the first part of the Fatima secret). As happened in the first days of Medjugorje, the visionaries were subjected to ridicule and harassment by the authorities, both civil and religious.

There were also great signs given to prove that the Virgin was truly appearing. The most remarkable was the first recorded miracle of the sun. In a dazzling display seen in the midst of a violent rainstorm, the sun seemed to move about the sky, spinning and dancing and appearing to come directly at the people. Many believed that it was the end of the world. Most convincing was the fact that a crowd numbering more than 70,000, including skeptics and journalists, witnessed the phenomenon firsthand. Thousands more saw it in areas surrounding the sight as far away as fifty miles.

Amazingly, when it was over, the skies had cleared, the sun shone brightly, and all present were amazingly dry and free of the mud that had previously caked their clothing. Believers and unbelievers alike were astonished.

Fatima is undoubtedly the most prophetic of modern apparitions. The first and second parts of the "secret" refer especially to the frightening vision of hell, devotion to the Immaculate Heart of Mary, the Second World War, and finally the prediction of the immense damage that Russia would do to humanity by abandoning the Christian faith and embracing Communist totalitarianism.

After the vision of hell, the children raised their frightened eyes beseechingly to the Virgin who told them: *You saw hell where the souls of poor sinners go. In order to save them, God wishes to establish in the world devotion to my Immaculate Heart. If people do what I ask, many souls will be saved and there will be peace. The war is going to end. But if people do not stop offending God, another, even worse, will begin in the reign of Pius XI.*

World War II would be the fulfillment of this prophecy. Fulfilled also was the promised sign of the war's proximity: a light seen around the world. That sign occurred in 1939 with the appearance of a strange, worldwide light in the sky, which many reported as resembling an aurora borealis. According to Lucia in an interview years later, this remarkable celestial event was not an aurora borealis, but a specific phenomenon predicted by the Madonna.

The Virgin proved herself true again on the subject of Russia: *. . . if people attend to my requests, Russia will be converted and the world will have peace. If not, Russia will spread its errors throughout the world, fomenting wars and persecutions of the Church . . .* And so it came to pass. The chaos in Russia developed into full revolution, leading to the full political development of atheistic Communism and its subsequent spread throughout the world. A little more than seventy years later, the Soviet Union would collapse without revolution or war. No worldly explanation seemed sufficient. Yet, those who believe in the Fatima messages remembered that its fall had been predicted.

The Blessed Virgin then gave Lucia what has come to be known as the third secret of Fatima. Actually, the so-called third secret is a continuation of the one secret quoted above. This particular part of the message was not to be revealed by the hierarchy of the Catholic Church until 1960. When the time came, however, it was decided not to release the secret out of concern over public reaction to its contents.

Then, on May 13, 2000, the anniversary of the Fatima apparitions, the Pope unexpectedly announced—not coincidentally—that the secret would be released within days. The long expected event came on June 26—the day after the nineteenth anniversary of the apparitions of Medjugorje.

Here is the third part of the Fatima secret in Lucia's own words, taken from a written statement she was ordered to write by the bishop of Elyria-Fatima in January 1944: "After the two parts which I have already explained, at the left of Our Lady and a little above, we saw an Angel with a flaming sword in his left hand; flashing, it gave out flames that looked as though they would set the world on fire; but they died out in contact with the splendour that Our Lady radiated towards him from her right hand. Pointing to the earth with his right hand, the Angel cried out in a loud voice: 'Penance! Penance! Penance!' And we saw in an immense light that is God: (something similar to how people appear in a mirror when they pass in front of it) a Bishop dressed in White (we had the impression that it was the Holy Father). Other Bishops, Priests, men and women Religious were going up a steep mountain, at the top of which there was a big Cross of rough-hewn trunks as of a cork-tree with the bark; before reaching there the Holy Father passed through a big city half in ruins and half trembling with halting step, afflicted with pain and sorrow, he prayed for the souls of the corpses he met on his way; having reached the top of the mountain, on his knees at the foot of the big Cross he was killed by a group of soldiers who fired bullets and arrows at him, and in the same way there died one after another the other Bishops, Priests, men and women Religious, and various lay people of different ranks and positions. Beneath the two arms of the cross, there were two Angels each with a crystal aspersorium in his hand, in which they gathered up the blood of the Martyrs and with it sprinkled the souls that were making their way to God."

The scene depicted in the third part of the secret is a stark review of the history of the Church during the past century. It is also a blunt warning to the people of the world, showing where we have been and where we are headed if we do not return to God.

To understand the signs of the times means to accept the urgency of penance—of conversion. It is reported that Sister Lucia, in a private conversation, said that it appeared ever more clearly to her that the purpose of all the apparitions was to help people to grow more and more in faith, hope and love. It could be added further that the apparitions of the Blessed Virgin also prepare her "children," as the Virgin refers to us at Medjugorje, for the time of final harvest when we are asked to choose between God and the world.

In a commentary on the entire secret, the head of the Congregation for the Doctrine of Faith of the Catholic Church, Joseph Cardinal Ratzinger, states that the "angel with the flaming sword on the left of the Mother of God recalls similar images in the Book of Revelation. This represents the threat of judgment, which looms over the world." However, he goes on to point out: "The future is not in fact unchangeably set, and the image which the children saw is in no way a film preview of a future in which nothing can be changed."

It seems the Cardinal has hit the nail directly on the head: the whole point of any such supernatural event or apparition or locution is to bring about a positive change in the individual soul; it is meant to guide us in the right direction without impeding our gift of free will.

More than sixty years after her startling appearances in Fatima, the Virgin has come to Medjugorje. We can see now that all earlier apparitions were merely a preparation for the messages of Medjugorje, the final messages that heaven is sending through the gracious intercession of the Mother of God. If we have learned well from this preparation, we will believe what she is telling us, transform our lives, and hold on to the hope that is promised.

Is there not enough proof that this is so? The predictions of La Salette came to pass just as the Virgin said. So, too, the prophecies of Fatima. So far, the apparitions of Medjugorje have followed the same pattern: the Virgin's unheeded plea for reconciliation resulted in a bloody civil war. Since then, she has repeatedly called for peace in the world through prayer, fasting, and a conversion of heart and life. Can we dare to ignore her warnings?

But the definitive proof that Medjugorje is in line with La Salette and Fatima lies at the core of these warnings and prophecies: the plan of heaven to save souls.

Certainly, the most poignant event in the Fatima apparitions was the vision of hell. Moved with pity, the children described the fall of "the souls of poor sinners." They were told why they had been exposed to this terrifying scene: "in order to save souls"—to show the way to salvation. In the Vatican's interpretation of the entire Fatima secret, "to save souls" is the key to the first and second parts of the secret, while the third part is summed up in the cry: "Penance, Penance, Penance!"

The children of Medjugorje have also been given a vision of hell, along with purgatory and heaven, for the same reason as the children of Fatima: to exhort them to prayer and penance for the salvation of souls.

In early October 1981, Vicka was at Jakov's home when the Virgin suddenly appeared and told them that she was going to take them to see heaven. Jakov, frightened and thinking they would not return said, "Why don't you just take Vicka. She has many brothers and sisters but I am the only child of my mother."

The Virgin smiled and took the two of them by the hand. In a flash, they were in heaven. Jakov's mother would report afterward that they completely disappeared from the house for a period of approximately twenty minutes. Vicka later described Heaven as a wonderfully beautiful place, filled with a sense of peace and happiness that made them want to stay and not return to earthly life. She said that it was filled with people dressed in pastel-colored gowns with no one older than thirty-three years of age. After showing them this part of paradise and telling them not to be afraid, the Virgin said: *All those who are faithful to God will have that.*

The visionaries described purgatory as a place of gray-brown mist, where they did not actually see anyone but felt anguish and yearning for peace. Vicka gave a frightening story as she described seeing hell as a place of fire and darkness. She reported vividly witnessing a teenage blond girl going into what appeared to the visionaries to be the flames of hell, shrieking and cursing God, coming out blackened and looking like an animal and continuing to curse God.

They questioned the Virgin about her reasons for showing them these places, especially paradise. *I did that so you could see the happiness, which awaits those who love God.* Suddenly, Jesus appeared to them in apparition, with injuries covering His body and wearing a crown of thorns. The Blessed Virgin comforted them. *Do not be afraid. It is my Son. See how He has been martyred. In spite of all, He was joyful and He endured all with patience.* The Virgin added: *I am often at Krizevac, at the foot of the cross, to pray there. Now I pray to my Son to forgive the world its sins. The world has begun to convert.*

During this apparition, the Virgin disappeared and the visionaries again saw a terrifying vision of hell. She then reappeared and said: *Do not be afraid! I have shown you hell so that you may know the state of those who are there.* She added: *The devil is trying to conquer us. Do not permit him. Keep the faith, fast, and pray. I will be with you at every step.* The Virgin was indescribable and beautiful light radiated, flowed, shined, and sparkled around her as she again added, *The people have begun to convert.*

Keep a solid faith. I need your prayers.

All the supernatural phenomena, all the prophecies and the promise of a permanent sign—every single wonder that has surrounded the Medjugorje apparitions—has been given for this one end: to bring men and women back to God in the final harvest of souls.

Lucia, now a cloistered nun in Portugal, is the only living visionary of Fatima. The Virgin had told her that she would live to see the Triumph of her Immaculate Heart. It is reported that upon hearing about Medjugorje, Lucia exclaimed that it is the fulfillment of the secrets of Fatima.

. . . . .

As the outcome of your faith you obtain the salvation of your souls.   1 Peter: 9

Chapter 9

An Army of Priests

In the last chapter we considered the connection between past Marian apparitions and their fulfillment in Medjugorje. However, just nine years before the Virgin's appearance at Medjugorje, another series of powerful messages began and continued nearly concurrently with the events of Medjugorje. These messages are strikingly parallel in nature and give further proof that Medjugorje is a culmination of the work of the Mother of God towards a final harvest of souls.

In May 1972, an Italian priest named Father Stefano Gobbi was taking part in a pilgrimage to Fatima. As he prayed for some priests who had left the priesthood and were forming into a rebellious group to challenge Church authority, he suddenly felt an interior presence of the Blessed Virgin Mary. From that point, he began receiving interior locutions from her, a series of powerful, blunt messages designed to recruit priests for these end times, a formation that would become a loosely organized "army of priests" known as the Marian Movement of Priests.

For more than twenty-five years, Father Gobbi traveled the globe speaking at assemblies of priests about the messages. Today, close to 4,000 priests, including twenty bishops, are members of the Marian Movement of Priests. The public cenacles came to an end in 1998, as the Blessed Virgin stated that she had said all that is necessary . . .

After everything we have described so far, is it any wonder that this phenomenon began at Fatima? At the same time, the general theme of the messages given to Father Gobbi is nearly identical to that of Medjugorje. The only difference is in the tone of the messages: blunt and pointed, as opposed to simple and tender, as at Medjugorje. But Medjugorje's lessons are meant for the faithful, the children of God; the Marian Movement of Priests is meant for those ordained to the sacred ministry and care of the Church, to alert them in the strongest possible terms and give them encouragement.

The echo of Fatima is always present in the messages received by Father Gobbi. Consider these words, given—not coincidentally—on May 13, 1990, the anniversary of the Fatima apparitions, in the very place where the Virgin had appeared: *I came down from heaven seventy-three years ago, in this Cova da Iria, to point out for you the path you should tread in the course of this difficult century of yours . . . Humanity has not accepted my motherly request to return to the Lord along the road of conversion of heart and of life, of prayer and of penance. Thus, it has known terrible years of the second world war, which brought about tens of millions of deaths and vast destruction of populaces and of nations . . . Satan has been the uncontested dominator of the events of this century of yours, bringing all humanity to the rejection of God and of His law of love, spreading far and wide division and hatred, immorality and wickedness and legitimating everywhere divorce, abortion, obscenity, homosexuality and recourse to any and all means of obstructing life . . . I am coming down from heaven [now, in these times] so that the final secrets may be revealed to you and that I may be able thus to prepare you for what, as of now, you must live through, for the purification of the earth . . .*

Again, as we saw in the last chapter, predicted chastisements are changeable with obedience to the Blessed Virgin's requests. It should be noted that she states "as of now," indicating that what is to come can be altered by humanity's response.

Always the loving mother, the Blessed Virgin ends the message on a note of hope: *Humanity will live through the moment of its great chastisement and thus will be made ready to receive the Lord Jesus who will return to you in glory . . .*

And this in conclusion: *For this reason, especially today, I am coming down again from heaven: through my numerous apparitions; through the messages which I give; and, through this extraordinary work of my Marian Movement of Priests, to prepare you to live through the events which are even now in the process of being fulfilled, in order to lead you by the hand to walk along the most difficult and painful segment of this your second advent, and to prepare the minds and the hearts of all to receive Jesus at the closely approaching moment of His glorious return.*

In short, the messages of the Marian Movement of Priests are confirmation of the Fatima apparitions; they are virtually the same in general content as the messages given at La Salette. The Virgin herself affirmed this by a message given on—what else?— the anniversary of Fatima, May 13, 1987: . . . *[B]ut now you are beginning to live through what I foretold to you in Fatima for the last years of this century of yours* . . . And again, the most powerful confirmation of all, given on May 13, 1991: . . . *You feel yourselves to be very united spiritually to my Pope John Paul II, this precious gift which my Immaculate Heart has made to you and who, in these very moments, is at prayer in the Cova da Iria, in order to thank me for the motherly and extraordinary protection which I gave him, saving his life on the occasion of the bloody attack, which took place ten years ago in St. Peter's Square. Today, I confirm that this is the Pope of My secret; the Pope of whom I spoke to the children during the apparitions . . .*[7]

The apparitions of La Salette and Fatima demonstrate that God always pours out special grace on humanity in times of crisis. Now, in the darkest of times, He continues do so at Medjugorje, once again through the intercession of His mother, our mother. She brings us grave warnings, but always with the consolation of the inevitable triumph of God over evil. Consider these words, taken from a message given to Father Gobbi on May 13, 1993: . . . *[F]rom the chalice of sufferings never before experienced, there will come forth the divine sun of a new era, never before known by humanity, of grace and holiness, love and justice, joy and peace* . . .

. . . . .

And when Elizabeth heard the greeting of Mary, the babe leaped in her womb; and Elizabeth was filled with the Holy Spirit and she exclaimed with a loud cry, "Blessed are you among women, and blessed is the fruit of your womb! And why is this granted me, that the mother of my Lord should come to me?"

Luke 1:41-43

---

7. Emphasis added. See the text of the third part of the Fatima secret in the previous chapter.

Chapter 10

More Confirmation

As she had done during her appearances at La Salette and Fatima, and in her messages through the Marian Movement of Priests, the Virgin implored the Medjugorje visionaries, villagers, and pilgrims to focus on the content of the grace she was bringing them through her messages. She reminded them again of the threat of Satan: *Satan only says what he wants. He interferes in everything. You, my angels, be ready to endure everything. Here, many things will take place. Do not allow yourselves to be surprised by him.*

The most insistent questions posed by pilgrims and clergy alike were theological in nature. The Virgin responded explicitly, giving even more information than she had at Fatima. To one inquiry concerning purgatory, she answered: There are many souls in purgatory. *There are also persons [there] who have been consecrated to God—some priests, some religious. Pray for their intentions, at least the Lord's Prayer, the Hail Mary, and the Glory Be seven times each, and the Creed. I recommend it to you. There is a large number of souls who have been in purgatory for a long time because no one prays for them.*

In another message, Ivanka was told this about purgatory: In purgatory there are different levels; the lowest is close to hell and the highest gradually draws near to heaven. It is not on All Souls Day, but at Christmas, that the greatest number of souls leave purgatory. There are in purgatory, souls who pray ardently to God, but for whom no relative or friend prays on earth. God makes them benefit from the prayers of other people. It happens that God permits them to manifest themselves in different ways, close to their relatives on earth, in order to remind men of the existence of purgatory and to solicit their prayers to come close to God who is just, but good. The majority of people go to purgatory. Many go to hell. A small number go directly to heaven.

Some people were disturbed that someone who was "bad" all their life could suddenly repent and be loved by God. The visionaries, at the request of one such person, asked the Virgin about being bad all one's life and asking forgiveness: *Whoever has done very much evil during his life can go straight to heaven if he confesses, is sorry for what he has done, and receives Communion at the end of his life.*

And concerning hell for those who do not repent: *Today many persons go to hell. God allows His children to suffer in hell due to the fact that they have committed grave, unpardonable sins. Those who are in hell no longer have a chance to know a lot better.*

Other answers stated that people who commit grave sins live in hell while still on earth and continue this hell in eternity, meaning they reject God completely and consciously choose evil as a life style. They actually go to hell because they chose it in life, and at the moment of death.

Mirjana shared with her spiritual advisor that she felt such an overwhelming, intimate experience of the Blessed Virgin's maternal love, that she could not understand how any soul could choose to go to hell. She questioned Gospa as to why God could so "mercilessly" send sinners to hell forever. The Blessed Virgin answered with gentleness: *Men who go to hell no longer want to receive any benefit from God. They do not repent nor do they cease to revolt and to blaspheme. They make up their mind to live in hell and do not contemplate leaving it.*

The Virgin revealed this startling information about heaven and reincarnation: *You go to heaven in full conscience—that which you have now. At the moment of death, you are conscious of the separation of the body and soul. It is false to teach people that you are reborn many times and that you pass to different bodies. One is born only once. The body, drawn from the earth, decomposes after death. It never comes back to life again. Man receives a transfigured body.*

Of course, there were constant questions and requests for cures for physical conditions and sicknesses. To one such question, she replied: *For the cure of the sick, it is important to say the following prayers: the Creed, and seven times each, The Lord's Prayer, the Hail Mary, and the Glory Be, and to fast on bread and water. It is good to impose one's hands on the sick and to pray. It is good to anoint the sick with Holy oil. All priests do not have the gift of healing. In order to receive this gift, the priest must pray with perseverance and believe firmly.*

This sequence of prayers taught to the visionaries in the first days of the apparitions and recommended frequently by the Blessed Virgin seems to be a powerful formula. It's simplicity points to one of the fundamental graces of her visit in Medjugorje: she brings us back to the basics and reminds us that it is only through prayer and fasting that heaven responds.

How do we fast? Who must fast and what is the best way? Her response: *The best fast is on bread and water. Through fasting and prayer, one can stop wars, one can suspend the laws of nature. Charity cannot replace fasting. Those who are not able to fast can sometimes replace it with prayer, charity, and a confession; but everyone, except the sick, must fast.*

In fasting, the Virgin is asking for the people to give God a gift. Sometimes, it is a large gift and other times a small one. Some days we are able to fast on bread and water, and other days we cannot; thus, the gift is smaller. What is important, she emphasizes, is that we attempt to give a gift. If one cannot fast on bread and water, for example, due to sickness or handicap, one can give up normal pleasures, such as TV, shopping, sweets, etc. That gift, combined with prayers, can then be "used" by heaven to answer the needs of others and encourage them towards a more spiritual life.

The Virgin makes a similar point concerning confession: *One must invite people to go to Confession each month, especially the first Saturday.[8] Here, I have not spoken of it yet. I have invited people to frequent Confession. I will give you yet some concrete messages for our time. Be patient because the time has not yet come. Do what I have told you. They are numerous who do not observe it. Monthly Confession will be a remedy for the Church in the West. One must convey this message to the West.*

---

8. At Fatima, the Blessed Virgin asked for a special devotion on the first Saturday of the month, consisting of the full fifteen decade rosary, confession, and Mass.

As to her role as a messenger from heaven: *I do not dispose all graces. I receive from God what I obtain through prayer. God has placed His complete trust in me. I particularly protect those who have been consecrated to me. The great sign has been granted. It will appear independently of the conversion of the people.*

On praying to her, the Blessed Virgin Mary makes clear her role and that of other saints: *Jesus prefers that you address yourselves directly to Him rather than through an intermediary. In the meantime, if you wish to give yourselves completely to God, and if you wish that I be your protector, then confide to me all your intentions, your fasts, and your sacrifices so that I can dispose of them according to the will of God. In other words, she intercedes for us, just as we ask one another to pray for our needs.*

On questions concerning the world: Would there be a third world war? *The third world war will not take place.* What will happen in Poland where the people have been fighting for freedom for so long? *There will be great conflicts, but in the end, the just will take over.* And what about Russia? *The Russian people will be the people who will glorify God the most. The West has made civilization progress, but without God, as if they were their own creators.*

. . . . .

In December 1982, there was a sharp change in the routine of the apparitions. For a year and a half now, the Madonna had come daily, appearing to each of the six visionaries. As already related, she had told them that she would give them ten secrets concerning the future of the world, and upon receiving the tenth, they would no longer see her daily. For Mirjana, that final apparition would come too soon. In late December, the Virgin told her: *On Christmas, I will appear to you* [daily] *for the last time.*

Mirjana was given the tenth secret and later reported that it was a particularly grave one. Also, while the Virgin would no longer be appearing to her every day, she promised to appear on Mirjana's birthday, March 18, for the rest of her life, as well as at other times when necessary. The final daily apparition lasted forty-five minutes. Mirjana stated that she will always remember these words of Our Lady: *Now you will have to turn to God in the*

57

faith like any other person. I will appear to you on the day of your birthday and when you will experience difficulties in life. Mirjana, I have chosen you; I have confided in you everything that is essential. I have shown you many terrible things. You must now bear it all with courage. Think of me and think of the tears I must shed for that. You must remain courageous. You have quickly grasped the messages. You must also understand now that I have to go away. Be courageous.

It was a sad Christmas for Mirjana. She later reported in an interview: "After she left, I just sat there like a statue, feeling very strange and thinking to myself: 'This can't be happening, she will come back.'"

But she did not come back. After calming down in the next few days, Mirjana added, "Our Lady said that she has stayed with us for longer than necessary, because this is the last time Jesus or she will appear on earth."[9]

Mirjana's final apparition left the five remaining visionaries wondering how much longer the Madonna of Medjugorje would appear to them.

. . . . .

For he will render to every man according to his works: to those who by patience in well-doing seek for glory and honor and immortality, he will give eternal life; but for those who are factious and do not obey the truth, but obey wickedness there will be wrath and fury.   Romans 2:6-8

---

9. Meaning, in apparition.

Chapter 11

New Dimension

The Blessed Virgin Mary added a new dimension to the apparitions at Medjugorje as they continued into 1983. A ten-year-old girl from the village suddenly began seeing and hearing the Blessed Virgin in a fashion different from the visionaries. She began "hearing" the Virgin interiorly, just as Father Gobbi of the Marian Movement of Priests heard her. Coming as it did a few days after Mirjana received her final daily apparition, it was almost certainly not coincidence.

While in class at school, Jelena Vasilij began hearing a gentle voice speaking to her interiorly. The words were of routine things at first, as though allowing the child to familiarize herself with the process. A few days later, Jelena discovered the "source" of the inner voice: "I saw and heard the angel who prepared me for the coming of Our Lady . . . He didn't say so, but I knew he was my guardian angel."

The Blessed Virgin first came to Jelena on December 29. She spoke but did not appear to her at first. When she did appear, it was in a different way than that of the six visionaries. Jelena described it as inner words and visions. She saw "with the heart" whereas the other six visionaries see the same thing with shut or open eyes. Also, Jelena's locutions occurred two or three times in a day. She would prepare as the visionaries did with a period of prayer.

Three months later, another ten-year-old, and close friend of Jelena, who was frequently in prayer with her before her locutions, began experiencing the same charism. Marijana Vasilij (not related) became the eighth youth in the village to experience the presence of Gospa. She would later describe to a priest how the young locutionists saw her (curiously, different in her manner of coming and her attire): "First a white cloud comes that disappears when Our Lady comes. She is all in white and wears a crown of stars held together by themselves 'without a wire,' and a rosary hangs from her folded hands."

Marijana also stated that Jesus sometimes accompanied the Virgin during the interior visions. She described Him as being seen only from the waist up, having long black hair and wearing a gray robe with a red cape.[10] She added that He was only seen and never spoke during these sessions, although He sometimes smiled.

In May 1983, the Virgin began giving Jelena teachings concerning the spiritual life. She told her to write the teachings down because she was to entrust them later to Church authorities. By this time, Jelena, who was the main receiver of the inner locutions, could speak to the Virgin at will—but only on spiritual matters. The Blessed Virgin told her that all she needs to know is written in the Gospels, that she should read and believe it, and that she would find all the answers there.

While the mission of these two young people receiving locutions is complementary to that of the six visionaries, they were told it would be different later. They would not receive the special future event messages (the ten secrets) that were to be given to the others, but they seemed to receive stronger, more detailed messages of spirituality. Still, their role was not quite on the same spiritual plane as the visionaries.

After four months of preparing her two children, the Blessed Virgin asked Jelena to advise her spiritual director that she would like a prayer group in the parish comprised of young people. Guidelines given by Gospa asked members to voluntarily commit to four years of total consecration to God, putting aside all decisions concerning the future during this time. They were asked to meet three times a week, to pray at least three hours daily, go to Mass frequently, and fast on bread and water twice a week. These guidelines would in time become the standard for similar prayer groups throughout the world, inspired by the apparitions at Medjugorje.

The first meeting took place in the basement of the rectory on

---

10. This description of Jesus by the locutionist is slightly different from that given by the visionaries where he is described as having "brown" hair.

a Tuesday evening. Interestingly, the Virgin's first message to the group was to love their enemies: *I know that you are not able to love your enemies, but I beg you to pray every day at least five minutes to the Sacred Heart, and to my Heart, and we will give you the divine love with which you will be able to love even your enemies.*

As had been the case in the first year and a half of apparitions, the Blessed Virgin again emphasized prayer as a pathway to learning spiritual love. And again, she pointedly reminded the people of the ethnic divisions within the region. Such a message was especially important to the young who are potentially more capable of changing traditional hatreds than adults who have had them ingrained from decades of conflict.

The young people's prayer group grew in spiritual intensity and in numbers. Two months later, the Madonna told the group: *You have decided to follow Jesus, to consecrate yourselves totally to Him. Now, when a person decides to follow God totally, Satan comes along and tries to remove that person from the path on which they have set out. This is the time of testing. He will try by all means to lead you astray. Satan will tell you: 'This is too much. This is nonsense. You can be Christians like everybody else. Don't pray, don't fast.' I tell you, this is the time when you must persevere in your fast and your prayers. You must not listen to Satan. Do what I have told you. Satan can do nothing to those who believe in God and have totally abandoned themselves to him. But you are inexperienced and so I urge you to be careful.*

. . . . .

As the year progressed, Ivan, Jakov, Marija, and Vicka related the following information to their spiritual director: Marija had received seven of the promised ten secrets; Vicka had received eight, while Jakov, Ivanka, and Ivan had nine each. Mirjana had all ten, of course, and no longer received daily apparitions.

For many of the pilgrims coming to the village, the main focus was still on the externals—the signs and wonders—more so than on the contents of the messages. It seemed that almost daily the visionaries were asked about the permanent sign. Again, the Virgin relayed information about the permanent sign: *The sign will come; you must not worry about it. The only thing that I would*

*want to tell you is to be converted. Make that known to all my chil-
dren as quickly as possible. No pain, no suffering is too great for
me in order to save you. I will pray to my Son not to punish the
world; but I plead with you, be converted. You cannot imagine
what is going to happen nor what the Eternal Father will send to
earth. That is why you must be converted! Renounce everything.
Do penance. Express my thanks to all my children who have
prayed and fasted. I carry all this to my Divine Son in order to
obtain an alleviation of His justice against the sins of mankind. I
thank the people who have prayed and fasted. Persevere and help
me to convert the world.*

The number of priests visiting the village constantly increased,
and with them came more serious questions. Regarding inquiries
concerning the physical healing taking place at Medjugorje, the
Virgin reminded again: *I cannot cure. God alone cures. Pray! I
will pray with you. Believe firmly. Fast, do penance. I will help you
as long as it is in my power to do it. God comes to help everyone.
I am not God. I need your sacrifices and your prayers to help me.*

Such messages added dramatically to the credibility of the
apparitions. Opposition continued, but in ratio to the conversions
taking place daily, it was all but overshadowed. This was especially true among visiting religious. Many priests were astounded
to find themselves spending literally hours hearing confessions.
Lines formed all over the outside lawn and in adjoining open
areas. The depth and intensity of these confessions caused many
priests who had come as skeptics to accept and believe that the
Virgin was appearing in Medjugorje.

. . . . .

The second anniversary of the apparitions, June 25, 1983,
passed with little fanfare. There was no special message given by
the Virgin to mark the event, but the visionaries did reveal that the
Virgin was giving them her life's story. They said it could not be
released until she gave the word. Vicka, it seemed, was the main
recipient of this privileged information; over nearly four months
she filled three notebooks.

Opposition by the local bishop, Pavao Zanic, remained the
biggest problem. Stirred by the continuing feud between secular

and Franciscan priests in his diocese, Bishop Zanic was now the most vocal active opponent. The situation was worsened by the ongoing threats of jail—or worse—from government authorities if the bishop did not put an end to what they described as "nonsense." The bishop was doing his best to comply.

When the problem of the bishop was brought to the Virgin's attention by the visionaries, she responded: *Fast two days a week for the intentions of the Bishop, who bears a heavy responsibility. If there is a need to, I will ask for a third day. Pray each day for the Bishop.*

In August, Jakov questioned the Virgin concerning orders from the bishop to have Father Tomislav Pervan, now the parish priest, stop the visionaries from saying the rosary and the Lord's Prayer, the Hail Mary, and the Glory Be the customary seven times at the beginning of prayer: *If it is so, then do not go against it so as not to provoke any quarrels. If it is possible, talk about it tomorrow among yourselves. All of you come to an agreement beforehand.*

Later, in the same month, she added: *Pray more for your spiritual life. Do your utmost in this sense. Pray for your Bishop. This theme remained a constant in the messages: Pray. When I give you this message, do not be content to just listen to it. Increase your prayer and see how it makes you happy. All graces are at your disposal. All you have to do is to gain them. In order to do that, I tell you—pray!*

In October, she admonished them with this message: *My Son suffers very much because men do not want to be reconciled. They have not listened to me. Be converted, be reconciled. And again later in the same month: The important thing is to pray to the Holy Spirit so that He may descend on you. When one has Him, one has everything. People make a mistake when they turn only to the saints to request something. Begin by calling on the Holy Spirit each day. The most important thing is to pray to the Holy Spirit. When the Holy Spirit descends on earth, then everything becomes clear and everything is transformed. I know that many will not believe you, and that many who have an impassioned faith will cool off. You remain firm, and motivate people to instant prayer, penance, and conversion. At the end, you will be happier.*

The mother of Jesus was making it clear that she was there to harvest every possible soul for her Son. She appeared determined to stay in Medjugorje until the goal was accomplished.

. . . . .

For God so loved the world that he gave his only Son, that whoever believes in him should not perish but have eternal life. For God sent the Son into the world, not to condemn the world, but that the world might be saved through him.   John 3:16-17

Chapter 12

Heaven's Plan

In November 1983, on direct instructions from the Blessed Virgin Mary, Mirjana gave her spiritual director an important synopsis of information concerning the apparitions. In essence, this synopsis was a general outline of why the Blessed Virgin Mary had been sent to Medjugorje. At the same time, it confirmed Medjugorje's connection with Fatima.

Nearly eighteen months of unprecedented, daily apparitions had continued without any indication of drawing to an end soon. This was far longer and more consistent than the seven months of sporadic visions that had taken place at Fatima. The impact of Medjugorje was being felt far beyond the borders of the little village in central Bosnia-Hercegovina. News of the mystical events at Medjugorje had spread swiftly, and pilgrims were now coming from all over the world. Scientists, medical experts, and theologians were constantly in the village, performing batteries of tests on the visionaries, or requesting to do so.

More importantly, the formation of a specific plan and purpose was becoming clear through the messages themselves. The information given to Father Vlasjic by Mirjana confirmed it. He was then asked by the Virgin through the visionary to convey this information to the Pope. Here is what he sent to Pope John Paul II in December 1983:

"During the apparition of December 25, 1982, according to Mirjana, the Madonna confided to her the tenth and last secret, and revealed to her the dates in which the different secrets will be realized. The Blessed Virgin revealed to Mirjana some aspects of the future up to this point in greater detail than to the other seers. For this reason, I am reporting here what Mirjana told me in a conversation of November 5, 1983.

I summarize the essentials of her account, without literal quotation. Mirjana told me that before the visible sign is given to mankind, there will be three warnings to the world. The warnings will be in the form of events on earth. Mirjana will be a witness to them. Ten days before one of the admonitions, Mirjana will notify a priest of her choice. The witness of Mirjana will be a confirmation of the apparitions and a stimulus for the conversion of the world.

After the admonitions, the visible sign will appear on the site of the apparitions in Medjugorje for all the world to see. The sign will be given as a testimony to the apparitions and in order to call people back to faith. The ninth and tenth secrets are serious. They concern chastisement for the sins of the world. Punishment is inevitable, for we cannot expect the whole world to be converted.

The punishment can be diminished by prayer and penance, but it cannot be eliminated. Mirjana says that one of the evils that threatened the world, the one contained in the seventh secret, has been averted thanks to prayer and fasting.[11] That is why the Blessed Virgin continues to encourage prayer and fasting (as she tells us): *You have forgotten that through prayer and fasting you can avert wars and suspend the laws of nature.*

After the first admonition, the others will follow in a rather short time. Thus, people will have some time for conversion. That interval will be a period of grace and conversion. After the visible sign appears, those who are still alive will have little time for conversion.

For that reason, the Blessed Virgin invites us to urgent conversion and reconciliation. The invitation to prayer and penance is meant to avert evil and war, but most of all to save souls. According to Mirjana, the events predicted by the Blessed Virgin are near. By virtue of this experience, Mirjana proclaims to the world: 'Convert as quickly as possible. Open your hearts to God.'

In addition to this basic message, Mirjana related an apparition she had in 1982, which we believe sheds some light on aspects of

11. A startling revelation by the Blessed Virgin, and verification that her call for prayer and fasting bears incredible fruits.

Church history. She spoke of an apparition in which Satan appeared to her. Satan asked Mirjana to renounce the Madonna and follow him. That way she could be happy in love and in life. He said that following the Virgin, on the contrary, would only lead to suffering. Mirjana rejected him, and immediately the Virgin gave her the following message, in substance: *Excuse me for this, but you must realize that Satan exists. One day he appeared before the throne of God and asked permission to submit the Church to a period of trial. God gave him permission to try the Church for one century.* **This century is under the power of the Devil, but when the secrets confided to you come to pass, his power will be destroyed.** *[emphasis added] Even now he is beginning to lose his power and has become aggressive. He is destroying marriages, creating division among priests, and is responsible for obsessions and murder. You must protect yourselves against these things through fasting and prayer, especially community prayer. Carry blessed objects with you. Put them in your house, and restore the use of holy water."*

Earlier, in a taped interview, Father Tomislav had made this comment: "The visionaries say that with the realization of the secrets entrusted to them by Our Lady, life in the world will change. Afterwards, men will believe like in ancient times. What will change and how it will change, we don't know, given that they don't want to say anything about the secrets."

. . . . .

Soon after this summation was completed and sent to the Pope, visionary Marija was given this message by the Virgin in response to a question by a priest: *You must warn the bishop very soon, and the Pope, with respect to the urgent and the great importance of the message for all mankind. I have already said many times that the peace of the world is in a state of crisis. Become brothers among yourselves; increase prayer and fasting in order to be saved. I know that many will not believe you, and that many who have an impassioned faith will cool off. You remain firm, and motivate people to instant prayer, penance, and conversion. At the end, you will be happier.*

There could now be little doubt about the urgency of the

appearances of the Blessed Virgin Mary in Medjugorje, or of their relationship to the apparitions at Fatima.

. . . . .

For every one who does evil hates the light, and does not come to the light, lest his deeds should be exposed. But he who does what is true comes to the light, that it may be clearly seen that his deeds have been wrought in God.   John 3: 20-21

Chapter 13

Growing Period

The young people's prayer group formed at the Blessed Virgin's request through Jelena was definitely a part of the overall plan of Medjugorje. It grew in spirit and dedication to the task, serving as an example for young and old alike. Jelena received a steady flow of messages and stated that the Virgin blessed her daily, adding: "When she comes to bless me, light flows from her hands. There is something special that emanates from her."

In May 1983, the Virgin began giving Jelena teachings concerning the spiritual life, asking her to write them down so that she could entrust them to the authorities of the Church at a later date. Some of the Franciscans thought that this might be the primary purpose of the locutionists' involvement in the events of Medjugorje. Especially the involvement of Jelena. Her messages were pointed and more direct, extremely similar to the messages of the Virgin given to Father Gobbi of the Marian Movement of Priests.

One of the most significant teachings by the Virgin was given to Jelena in November: *Begin by calling on the Holy Spirit each day. The most important thing is to pray to the Holy Spirit. When the Holy Spirit descends on earth, then everything becomes clear and everything is transformed.*

A few days later she directed Jelena to tell the group: *Pray! I am your mother full of goodness, and Jesus is your great friend. Do not fear anything in His presence. Give Him your heart, from the bottom of your heart. Tell Him your sufferings, thus, you will be invigorated in prayer, with a free heart, in a peace without fear.*

It was a new way of life for these young people. Time not spent working and doing family chores was now intense time for prayer and learning. The group included all of the visionaries and the two locutionists, with visionary Marija being the main one chosen to assist and meet with the prayer group regularly, helping them with messages and personal witness.

In late December, the Virgin gave this message to Jelena for the prayer group: *My children, pray! I cannot tell you anything else other than to pray. Know that in your life, there is nothing more important than prayer.*

As though to back up this brief message, she poured out a blunt and powerful message on the day after Christmas: *The Mass is the greatest prayer of God. You will never be able to understand its greatness. That is why you must be perfect and humble at Mass, and you should prepare yourselves there. There are many Christians who are no longer faithful, because they do not pray any more. Have them begin again to recite each day, at least, seven Our Father's, seven Hail Mary's, seven Glory Be's, and the Creed, once.*

Once again, the Virgin puts forth this simple formula of prayer; but she wasn't through with this particular lesson, one that would apply especially for the faithful in the west. She continued: *Above all, abstain from television programs. They represent a great peril for your families. After you have seen them, you cannot pray any more. Give up likewise alcohol, cigarettes, and pleasure of this kind.*

And of course, the "lesson" would not be complete without a request for fasting to go along with the prayer: *The fasting which you are doing in eating fish instead of meat, is not fasting but abstinence. The true fast consists in giving up all our sins, but one must also renounce himself, and make the body participate in it. Monthly confession will be a remedy for the Church in the West. Whole sections of the Church could be cured if the believers would go to confession once a month.*

She followed with this message in February: *Pray, pray! How many persons have followed other beliefs or sects and have abandoned Jesus Christ. They create their own gods; they adore idols. How that hurts me! If they could be converted! Like the unbelievers, they are many! That will change only if you help me with your prayers.*

Emphasis again is placed on the fact that all of the teachings initiated through the six visionaries and two locutionists were meant personally for them first and then the parish. Eventually, it was for everyone who would listen. This period was essentially a powerful time of learning in preparation for those who would come on pilgrimage to witness for themselves the grace being poured out in Medjugorje.

. . . . .

In March 1984, the Virgin took her preparatory work to the next level as she began giving personal weekly messages to the parish on Thursday evenings—as always, through visionary Marija. The teaching was now being expanded to the entire parish, as the Virgin stated in the first of the weekly messages to Marija: *Dear children! I have chosen this parish in a special way and I wish to lead it. I am guarding it in love and I wish everyone to be mine. Thank you for your response this evening. I wish that you will always be here in greater numbers with me and my Son. Every Thursday, I will give a special message to you. Thank you for your response to my call.*

The villagers were happily stunned at such personal attention from the Mother of Jesus. For several weeks, the church was filled to overflowing. Many men were also present and remained for longer periods of time, especially when there was Adoration of the Blessed Sacrament. It was a wonderful beginning to the new phase of messages.

March 25th marked another significant milestone in the apparitions. It was the 1,000th day of continuous apparitions at Medjugorje, a feat unprecedented in Marian history. The Blessed Virgin gave this startling message: *Rejoice with me and with my angels, because a part of my plan has already been realized. Many have been converted, but many do not want to be converted. Pray!* She then looked at the visionaries a long time and tears of happiness flowed down her cheeks. Three days later, in marked contrast, she said: *Many persons come here out of curiosity and not as pilgrims.*

In keeping with human nature, the enthusiasm of receiving such remarkable, personal teachings would soon wane. How could such a precious gift be taken for granted so quickly? Yet, such was the case. The Blessed Virgin's admonishments continued as crowds that only a few weeks before had filled the church dwindled. A personal message to one of the visionaries on April 5 was somber: *If you would be strong in the faith, Satan would not be able to do anything against you. Begin to walk the path of my messages. Be converted, be converted, be converted! And her weekly message for the parish that evening: Dear children, this evening I am especially asking you to venerate the heart of my Son, Jesus. Make atonement for the wounds inflicted to the heart of my Son. That heart has been offended with all sorts of sin. Thank you for coming this evening.*

Then, on Thursday, April 26, the Virgin gave no message. The small assembly of faithful villagers gathered in the church were saddened and puzzled. Marija concluded that, possibly, the Virgin was only giving the weekly message during Lent.

Several days later, Marija asked her: "Dear Lady, why have you not given me the message for the parish on Thursday?" The Virgin replied: *Even though I had a special message for the parish to awaken the faith of every believer, I do not wish to force anyone to anything he doesn't feel or doesn't want. Only a very small number have accepted the messages on Thursdays. At the beginning, there were more, but now it seems as if it has become something ordinary to them. And some have been asking recently for the message only out of curiosity, and not out of faith and devotion to my Son and me.*

Two weeks later, the church was once again filled: the people had responded to the Blessed Virgin's admonishment. With motherly assurance, the Queen of Peace told them: *I am still speaking to you and I intend to continue. Just listen to my instructions.*

The next two weeks brought further assurance that the Mother of God was there personally for everyone who would take the time to listen. On May 17 she said: *Dear children, today I am very happy because there are many who desire to devote themselves to me. I thank you! You have not made a mistake. My son, Jesus Christ, wishes to bestow on you special graces through me. My Son is happy because of your dedication.*

This was followed on May 24 with these loving words: *I have told you already that I have chosen you in a special way, the way you are. I, the Mother, love you all. And in any moment when it is difficult for you, don't be afraid. I love you even when you are far away from me and my Son. I ask you not to allow my heart to cry with tears of blood because of the souls who are being lost in sin. Therefore, dear children, pray, pray, pray!*

What greater grace could there be for a community than to have the Mother of God speaking to them weekly, guiding them to live a holy life, making each one feel as though she was speaking directly to them? This new grace was, of course, in addition to her regular daily appearance to the visionaries.

Within the context of the divine plan, the response of the community of Medjugorje was essential. From the faith and conversion of this tiny village, the whole world was to be given the opportunity to respond to the messages from heaven. Not only the visionaries, but every person in Medjugorje was of vital importance. Without them, in all probability, the plan would have failed.

. . . . .

Meanwhile, the "world" was there, conducting intensive investigations. Scientists, medical doctors, and theologians—whose personal feelings ranged from skeptical or curious, to simply unbelieving—continued to submit the visionaries to every possible kind of test. Even the crudest and most primitive kind of probes were included. Needles were stuck in the arms of Vicka while she was in ecstasy during the time of apparition, and tremendous noise was blasted into the ears of Ivan. Neither flinched, nor was there physical damage done to their senses. The Franciscans, however, soon put an end to such tests.

A strong argument for the genuineness of the apparitions, even stronger, perhaps, than the fact-gathering of scientists with their instruments, was the ordinariness of the visionaries. That was especially true with little Jakov, only ten years old when the apparitions commenced, and now, three years later, an impetuous thirteen-year-old boy. Jakov loved to joke and play; but during the apparitions, and when being questioned or tested by various authorities, he was well mannered, serious and straightforward with his answers.

However, at school he was all boy. One evening during the daily apparition, the Blessed Virgin reproached the young vision-ary because he had misbehaved toward some of the boys at school: You must love them all, she told him. Jakov then responded that he did love them but that they annoyed him and provoked him. Then accept it as a sacrifice, and offer it, she replied, most probably with an understanding, motherly smile.

When the visionaries, out of curiosity, again questioned the Virgin about how long the apparitions would continue, she answered, *Everything passes exactly according to God's plan. Have patience, persevere in prayer and in penance. Everything happens in its own time.*

Such simple but profound teachings; but always at the core of each message, the impetus to assure that heaven's plan through Medjugorje would be fulfilled.

. . . . .

I have yet many things to say to you, but you cannot bear them now. When the Spirit of truth comes, he will guide you into all the truth; for he will not speak on his own authority, but whatever he hears he will speak, and he will declare to you the things that are to come. John 16:12-13

Chapter 14

Heart of Medjugorje

In January 1985, the Blessed Virgin Mary gave a message which may be the most significant of all the messages she has given at Medjugorje. This is a strong statement considering the depth, scope, and daily impact of her apparitions at Medjugorje. Nonetheless, this one message, more than any other, epitomizes the very heart and soul of the Medjugorje phenomenon.

The impetus for the message came out of one man's expression of stubborn national pride, a poisonous pride that reached far beyond patriotism. This man was, sad to say, a priest of the Catholic faith who had difficulty understanding the healing of an Orthodox, gypsy child. How, he asked the visionaries, in obvious disgust and dismay, could the Mother of God intercede for the healing of this child of the faith of the despised ethnic enemy, the Serbians?

The question was put to the Virgin by one of the visionaries. She looked at the priest for a long time before answering. It was not a gaze of repulsion, as one might imagine in human terms; rather, it was that of a long-suffering mother with endless tolerance.

This was her response: *Tell this priest, tell everyone, that it is you who are divided on earth. The Muslims and the Orthodox, for the same reason as Catholics, are equal before my Son and me. You are all my children. Certainly, all religions are not equal, but all men are equal before God, as St. Paul says. It does not suffice to belong to the Catholic Church to be saved, but it is necessary to respect the commandments of God in following one's conscience.*

Those who are not Catholics, are no less creatures made in the image of God, and destined to rejoin someday the House of the Father. Salvation is available to everyone, without exception. Only those who refuse God deliberately are condemned. To him who has been given little, little will be asked for. To whomever has been given much, very much will be required. **It is God alone, in His infinite justice, who determines the degree of responsibility and pronounces judgment.** [emphasis added]

Never in three and a half years of daily messages had the Blessed Virgin Mary been so explicit concerning the divisions that existed in the country where God had chosen to send her. Here were years of tension coming to a head-on collision with God's truth. Even the trappings of the priesthood could not contain the nationalistic pride that would question the miraculous healing of a child.

At first glance, this message seems to address only the region of Bosnia-Hercegovina, torn by divisions of faith and ethnic backgrounds. Indeed, from her first conversation with the visionaries, the Blessed Virgin Mary had urgently appealed for reconciliation among the people of the region.

But her appeal was not meant for the small area of Bosnia-Hercegovina alone. As we have said before, Medjugorje is a microcosm of the world. In this message, given in direct address to a manifestation of national and religious pride—a destructive, divisive pride that would lead to violence and civil war—the Blessed Virgin Mary was addressing not just the region of Bosnia-Hercegovina, but the whole world. She was seeking to bring before the eyes of every man and woman the source of the divisions that threaten the lives and happiness of all. She was speaking words of wisdom for all her children, giving them the very heart of her reason for coming and staying with them for so long a time.

If only the people of Bosnia-Hercegovina had heeded the Virgin's words! But the message of reconciliation was too foreign, too unpalatable. Though many did struggle to rise above the rabid nationalism and ethnic prejudices that were tearing their land apart, though many did open their hearts to God, seeking to plant good spiritual seeds within their daily life, most unfortunately continued to foster age-old hatreds.

They would soon pay a horrible price for not taking seriously the Virgin's admonitions for reconciliation and peace. For a time it seemed that heaven's plan was doomed to tragic failure. It came painfully close.

Would the world fail to respond as well?

. . . . .

Why do you call me 'Lord, Lord,' and not do what I tell you? Every one who comes to me and hears my words and does them, I will show you what he is like: he is like a man building a house, who dug deep, and laid the foundation upon rock; and when a flood arose, the stream broke against that house, and could not shake it, because it had been well built. But he who hears and does not do them is like a man who built a house on the ground without a foundation; against which the stream broke, and immediately it fell, and the ruin of that house was great.

Luke 6:46-49

PART III

Fruits

So, every sound tree bears good fruit, but the bad tree bears evil fruit. A sound tree cannot bear evil fruit, nor can a bad tree bear good fruit. Every tree that does not bear good fruit is cut down and thrown into the fire. Thus you will know them by their fruits.

Matthew 7: 17-20

Chapter 15

More Change

In Medjugorje, it was a cold, blustery beginning to 1985. Yet, the hard-core faithful continued coming to Saint James Church for the evening prayers and apparition. There were no large bands of pilgrims who usually poured into Medjugorje from throughout the world. In the bitter-cold days of early January, those in attendance were mainly the villagers, well-accustomed to suffering such conditions. Of course, there was no heat in the church, and many were forced to remain outside in the harsh elements.

The Blessed Virgin graciously acknowledged their devotion: *I thank the faithful for having come to church in very bad and cold weather.*

She never failed to thank the people for enduring hardship to respond to her coming. And she always had words of encouragement and warning, as in this message: *My dear children, Satan is strong. He wishes with all his strength to destroy my plans. Pray only, and do not stop doing it. I will also pray to my Son so that all the plans that I have begun will be realized. Be patient and persevere in prayer. Do not permit Satan to take away your courage. He works very hard in the world. Be on your guard!*

Unknown to the people, ahead lay more changes, more challenges to the message they had received. It was important for the Virgin to let the people know the dangers, things as small as harsh weather, that could threaten to weaken their resolve. She showed herself willing to work with the parish of St. James, molding it personally and intimately into a paradigm of conversion and spiritual renewal. She was determined to attend to every detail to ensure that the work she had begun would take root and grow into a rich harvest.

To this end, Gospa expressed her desire that one of the Franciscan priests, Father Slavko Barbaric, who had served as the visionaries' spiritual advisor since July 1984, remain in the parish for a special work. She told the visionaries, *I wish for Father Slavko to stay here, to guide the life, and to assemble all the news so that when I leave, there will be a complete image of everything that has happened here. I am also praying now for Slavko, and for all those who work in this parish.*

It was an important message. Father Slavko, highly educated and able to communicate in seven languages, would see to it that there would be a systematic gathering of all pertinent data concerning the accurate recording and translation of the messages, the apparitions, as well as claimed cures. He would become in essence, the "caretaker" of Medjugorje's apparitions.

Ironically, Father Slavko was not assigned to the Medjugorje parish, and thus, had to travel daily to and from his parish approximately twenty-five miles away. But that little penance was representative of why he was the Virgin's choice for such an important task. He was involved in every aspect of the services offered at St. James, usually leading the rosary prayers each evening, mixing the many languages so that all could understand. Somehow he would always find time to hear confessions—again in the many different languages. He was everywhere and into everything, a source and a mountain of strength for all who came seeking the Father's love.

. . . . .

May 7, 1985, brought another major change in the Medjugorje phenomena. On this day, the Blessed Virgin told Ivanka, the first visionary to have seen her, that she would receive the tenth secret and, thus, no longer receive daily apparitions.

As with Mirjana, this was devastating news to the young woman. As the apparition ended, the other visionaries noticed that Ivanka remained in an unmoving state. For them, it was a shock to actually see one of their group in the state of ecstasy that occurred during each apparition. They saw her on her knees with eyes focused upwards on the spot where the Virgin was appearing. Ivanka spoke words, but no sounds came forth, and she seemed to be totally at peace.

That evening, the Blessed Virgin appeared again to Ivanka at her home for nearly an hour. She came flanked by two angels, compassionately asking her if she had any special requests. Ivanka asked to see her mother again. Within seconds, her mother appeared, hugged her and told her she was proud of her, and then disappeared. The Virgin then told Ivanka: *My dear child, today is our last meeting, do not be sad. I will return to see you at each anniversary of the first apparition, beginning next year. Dear child, do not think that you have done anything bad, and that this would be the reason why I'm not returning near to you. No, it is not that.*

With all your heart, you have accepted the plans which my Son and I formulated, and you have accomplished everything. No one in the world has had the grace which you, your brothers and sisters have received. Be happy because I am your mother and I love you from the bottom of my heart. Ivanka, thank you for the response to the call of my Son. Thank you for persevering and remaining always with Him as long as He will ask you.

Dear child, tell all your friends that my Son and I are always with them when they call on us. What I have told you during these years on the secrets, do not speak to anyone about them. Go in the peace of God.

Truly, Ivanka had responded well to the tremendous gift of grace of seeing the Blessed Virgin for so long a time. She had grown deeply spiritual and looked forward to life as a wife and mother. The gift of seeing her human mother again was as special a blessing as it had been the first time in the early days of the apparitions. She immediately withdrew as much as possible from the spotlight of being a visionary to begin living her new life.

Now there were only four visionaries receiving daily apparitions, while Jelena and Marijana continued to receive inner visions and locutions. Mirjana received occasional apparitions, as the Virgin had said she would, "in time of need," when the weight of the secrets and the ongoing charism would become too much. The Blessed Virgin would appear then to comfort her and sometimes give messages.

There was also a special role for Mirjana. She was the visionary selected to reveal the ten secrets through a priest of her choosing, and would be the only Medjugorje visionary with this responsibility. Mirjana chose a priest far from the parish and, when questioned about her choice, responded, "Gospa will take care of it." Shortly thereafter, Father Petar Ljubicic, whom Mirjana had selected, was assigned to the parish. The decision to transfer him was completely independent of the fact of Mirjana's choice.

.   .   .   .   .

In the latter part of 1985, the Virgin gave a series of messages pertaining directly to unbelievers, beginning with these words to Mirjana: *My angel, pray for unbelievers. People will tear their hair, brothers will plead with brothers, they will curse their past lives lived without God. They will repent, but it will be too late. Now is the time for conversion. I have been exhorting you for the past four years. Pray for them. Invite everyone to pray the rosary.*

And this message: *Those who say, 'I do not believe in God,' how difficult it will be for them when they will approach the throne of God and hear the voice: 'Enter into hell.'*

Again, concerning unbelievers: *They are my children. I suffer because of them. They do not know what awaits them. You must pray more for them.*

Such a string of messages concerning those who deliberately turn away from God shows again a Mother's love for all the world's children. As she had said so many times, she would be there for all, to the very last second of life. Even for the believer who stumbles and gives in to temptation, she had these reassuring words: *With respect to sin, it suffices to give it serious consideration, and soon, move ahead and correct the sin.* In short, to contritely ask forgiveness from God, to forgive oneself, and then get on with life.

The Virgin soon showed Mirjana the first of the ten secrets. The sight of such things, according to Mirjana, is "like watching a movie." Mirjana described seeing a place of desolation. The Madonna told her: It is the upheaval of a region of the world. In the world, there are so many sins. *What can I do, if you do not help me? Remember that I love you. God does not have a hard heart. Look around you and see what men do, then you will no* longer say that God has a hard heart. How many people come to church, to the house of God, with respect, a strong faith, and love God? Very few! Here you have a time of grace and conversion. It is necessary to use it well.

Such messages, accompanied by a powerful vision, were greatly disturbing to the visionaries; but, the Blessed Virgin often followed these difficult revelations with words such as these: *Have you forgotten that you are in my hands?*

. . . . .

And Mary said, "My soul magnifies the Lord, and my spirit rejoices in God my Savior, for he has regarded the low estate of his handmaiden. For behold, henceforth all generations will call me blessed; for he who is mighty has done great things for me, and holy is his name."   Luke 1:46-49

Chapter 16

Time of Mercy

In early 1986, much to the amazement of priests and pilgrims alike, Mirjana's role in the apparitions was unexpectedly revived. This event, like the addition of two locutionists to go along with the six visionaries, represented another striking departure from Fatima and other past apparitions.

For her part, Mirjana was not surprised. She was, after all, the visionary chosen to select a priest to reveal each secret as it was about to occur. This implied a certain on-going involvement. She began receiving a series of messages by inner locution, and occasional apparitions, which concerned the secrets and preparations for their occurrence. The Madonna began appearing or speaking to her interiorly on the second day of each month. The renewal of Mirjana's role continues as of this writing.

Was this an indication, as many thought, that the apparitions were coming to an end? That the secrets were about to be revealed? No, Mirjana stated, this was not the end of the apparitions. It was, rather, *a time of mercy*, a period of extra grace.

Even after four-plus years of extraordinary messages, the Queen of Peace continued to exhort her children to live the Gospel message of her Son. That exhortation was clearly evident as the daily apparitions continued with Marija, Vicka, Jakov, and Ivan, and in the personal, intimate messages for the people of the parish given to Marija every Thursday evening.

Medjugorje's apparitions, so much in form like those of Fatima, were different mainly because of their daily occurrence, longevity, and number of visionaries and locutionists involved. The unusual revival and emphasis of Mirjana's role concerning the secrets, added another dimension of difference. In retrospect, it could be understood as merciful guidance from heaven for a world bent on replacing the natural law of God with man-made civil law. Clearly, the Blessed Virgin Mary was pleading before the throne of God for just a little more time to reach all of her children.

As if to confirm once more that the time of mercy was still operative, the Virgin delivered this message just before the celebration of the fifth anniversary on June 25: *In these days, the Lord has allowed me to intercede for more graces for you. Therefore, dear children, I want to urge you once again to prayer. Pray constantly and, in this way, I will give you the joy which the Lord gives me. With these graces, dear children, I want your suffering to be for you a joy. I am your mother, and I want to help you.*

Late in the night of June 25, the Virgin gave this beautiful message to Ivan and Marija, which was later read to nearly one thousand pilgrims gathered on Podbrdo Hill: You are on a Thabor. You receive blessings, strength and love. Carry them into your families and into your homes. To each one of you, I grant a special blessing. Continue in joy, prayer and reconciliation.

This particular late-night message was important for me personally because I was present when it was given. It was during my first pilgrimage, and I vividly remember groping my way up Podbrdo Hill that night, joining a steady stream of pilgrims. No flashlights were allowed because the Communists had banned public gatherings on the hill. It was so dark you could hardly see the silhouette of the person directly in front of you. I huddled among the rocks in the darkness with thousands of other pilgrims, listening to these words from the Blessed Mother. The main thrust of her message that night was to pray with our families so that she could present us as, a beautiful flower that unfolds for her Son, Jesus . . .

Another powerful message of mercy was given August 4: *Read each Thursday the Gospel of Matthew, where it is said: 'No one can serve two masters . . . You cannot serve God and money.'* Later, her admonition to read this passage of Scripture each Thursday would translate into asking families to read it at least once a week as a regular reminder that all is in God's hands.

. . . . .

The extension of the time of mercy was highlighted again in January 1987, when the Blessed Virgin announced a change in her manner of giving messages: *Dear children! I want to thank you for every response to my call. I want to thank you for all the suffering and prayers you have offered to me. Dear children, I want to give you messages from now onwards no longer every Thursday, but on the 25th of each month. The time has come when what our Lord wanted has been fulfilled. From now on, I give you less messages but I will be with you. Therefore, dear children, I beg you to listen and to live my messages so I can guide you*

Again, the change was interpreted as a sign that the apparitions were winding down; any day now, it was thought by many followers, the Virgin would make her last appearance and give her final message. Again, the visionaries assured the public that no such notice was being given to them; it was simply another opportunity for grace.

Thus, on January 25, 1987, the Blessed Virgin began giving the new monthly messages through visionary Marija. As with the weekly messages, Marija would be the only one of the six to receive these special messages. From her comments and from the wording of the messages, it was evident that these texts were meant for wide publication so that they could reach everyone. On the 25th of each month, immediately following the apparition, Marija would write down the message and give it to Father Slavko Barbaric. It would then be thoroughly checked for adherence to Scripture and church doctrine, and in less than twenty-four hours, be transmitted to prayer groups and followers of Medjugorje around the world.

Other changes were taking place at a dizzying pace. The streets, fields, and homes of the villagers were now constantly filled with pilgrims. They were coming from every corner of the world. The Communist authorities, finally realizing their fears of insurrection were unfounded, began to change tactics. Now they were beginning to see Medjugorje as a new source of tourist income. The Virgin Mary was sarcastically referred to as "Our Lady of Currency." A new form of harassment commenced as authorities attempted to stop pilgrims from staying in individual homes and force them to stay in new, hastily built government accommodations.

But by this time, the flow of pilgrims was too large. The additional rooms constantly being added to the homes of villagers stayed filled in spite of newly passed local tax laws that demanded up to sixty-five percent of the income derived from private accommodations.

The harvest was now reaching far beyond the hills of Medjugorje.

.　.　.　.　.

No one can serve two masters; for either he will hate the one and love the other, or he will be devoted to the one and despise the other. You cannot serve God and mammon. Therefore I tell you, do not be anxious about your life, what you shall eat or what you shall drink, nor about your body, what you shall put on. Is not life more than food, and the body more than clothing? Look at the birds of the air; they neither sow nor reap nor gather into barns, and yet your heavenly Father feeds them. Are you not of more value than they? And which of you by being anxious can add one cubit to his span of life? And why are you anxious about clothing? Consider the lilies of the field, how they grow; they neither toil nor spin; yet I tell you, even Solomon in all his glory was not arrayed like one of these. But if God so clothes the grass of the field, which today is alive and tomorrow is thrown into the oven, will he not much more clothe you, O men of little faith? Therefore, do not be anxious, saying 'What shall we eat?' or 'What shall we drink?' or 'What shall we wear?' For the Gentiles seek all these things; and your heavenly Father knows that you need them all. But seek first His kingdom and His righteousness, and all these things shall be yours as well. Therefore, do not be anxious about tomorrow, for tomorrow will be anxious for itself. Let the day's own trouble be sufficient for the day. Matthew 6: 24-34

Chapter 17

The Call

The fifth anniversary of the apparitions arrived June 25, 1986, and everything seemed to be going according to heaven's plan. While the villagers had adjusted to the dramatic changes created by the Virgin's appearances among them, most aspects of daily life continued as before the apparitions.

Even the lives of the visionaries, open to constant public scrutiny, followed traditional patterns. Ivanka was now married and the mother of a little girl. She had quietly slipped into the background of village life, briefly coming into focus again when she announced plans to marry childhood friend Reyko Elez in June. How, the villagers and pilgrims alike asked, could she marry when the Virgin recommended a holy life for the visionaries as priests and nuns?

Ivanka was quick to answer. Yes, the Blessed Virgin did say it would be good if they pursued a religious vocation; she also said she would honor whatever course they chose, and, Ivanka added somewhat testily, "Marriage is also a sacrament of the Church!"

Ivan's life as a visionary was temporarily interrupted as he began a required one-year tour of military service. During a short period of adjustment to military life, the Virgin did not appear to him in apparition; instead, she spoke to him via inner locution. Only after he was settled into this new way of life did she begin reappearing in locations away from the barracks where he was stationed. On completion of his duty, the shy, introverted Ivan returned to the village matured, with a new confidence that became evident in his dealings with pilgrims. He now met frequently with pilgrim groups and answered their questions with calm and patience.

Mirjana had returned to Sarajevo for university studies, while Marija and Vicka took on the never-ending task of meeting with the increasing crowds of pilgrims. They would spend long hours each day patiently meeting with groups, answering the same questions repeatedly, and praying over the sick and handicapped. True to form, Jakov stayed away from the pilgrims except for his presence in the apparition room each evening. His days were filled with the carefree ways of a teenage boy.

Outwardly, new buildings dotted the landscape. Commercialism grew at rampant speed, and taxis roamed like a swarm of bees over decrepit bridges and dirt roads that were never intended to support such traffic. The roads were filled with pilgrims, and many villagers were busy adding extensions to their dwellings to house more pilgrims. For many villagers, the changes were uncomfortable annoyances offset only by the good fruits of the apparitions.

But more ominous changes were taking place on the world scene, changes that would heavily impact on the region where the Virgin had appeared daily now for five years.

From the first day, the Virgin had issued urgent warnings for the people to reconcile, pray and fast. For the most part, prayer and fasting became part of the daily life of the village. On Fridays, the popular day for fasting, it was all but impossible to get any type of meal that included meat in the restaurants, snack booths or homes where pilgrims stayed.

Still, the call for reconciliation was largely ignored, just as it had been at Fatima where the Virgin Mary had predicted in detail what would happen if the people of the world did not reconcile and pray. Nor did the recorded fulfillment of the Virgin's predictions at Fatima give any weight to the same daily miracle that was taking place at Medjugorje. Despite the Blessed Virgin's daily appearances and messages of peace, Croat, Serb, and Muslim refused to forget a lifetime of hating one another. Out of such obstinacy, the seeds of war began to take root.

As the fifth anniversary of the Medjugorje apparitions approached, Communism, that evil dragon that had for more than seventy years ruled a vast part of Eastern Europe, began to fall apart as masses of freedom-hungry people tore at its every limb. The fall of Communism was hailed with great enthusiasm, but soon it became clear that its dissolution had left many countries in a state of political and social turmoil. Wars of division raged within newly-freed countries, especially in the former Soviet Union, with many factions struggling for controlling power. Religious and ethnic persecution reached new heights in the blind fervor of an expanding ultra-nationalism.

The demise of the dragon originated in Poland and quickly spread into neighboring countries. The people of the oppressed nations making up the Federation of Yugoslavia, ruthlessly ruled and dominated by staunch Communists for more than forty years, finally saw a faint light of hope for true freedom. Many in Croatia and Bosnia-Hercegovina erroneously viewed the apparitions only as a sign that, at last, God had come to set them free from the political chains of oppression. It was a mistake, one made many times throughout history. In reality, the Yugoslav oppressors, predominantly Serbians, began making plans to maintain power.

With an evident sense of urgency, The Virgin's messages continued to appeal for her children to listen carefully and carry out her lessons. She knew what was about to happen if true conversion and reconciliation did not take place in the hearts of the people.

. . . . .

The apparitions had now developed into a major force for spiritual conversion. The story was reaching millions of people. In October 1985, it reached me. Two years later, I sat in the cool on the shady side of Saint James Church in Medjugorje, shaking at the thought that, shortly, I would be standing at the altar giving a talk to the English-speaking pilgrims.

Life had changed dramatically for me since my first encounter with the Medjugorje apparitions. Though I had heard "the Call" from God in the past, this was my first attempt to truly respond. It had come from a source totally foreign to me—the Blessed Virgin Mary, a woman of Scripture whom I had always thought to be only for Catholics.

No longer was success in business my prime motivation; now, I was driven to spread the message of Medjugorje, a message of renewal and hope, a reiteration of the Gospel. I was immersed in a busy schedule of national and international travel, telling the story of the apparitions, and witnessing what the Call had done to my life.

In the brief space of twenty months, I traveled to Medjugorje four times. I had spent many hours in this church listening to homilies and talks about the dramatic spiritual changes wrought in the lives of others by the daily apparitions. Now, I would be the one witnessing.

As usual, I had not prepared anything special for the talk. At the end, it was greeted with warm applause. Unbeknownst to me, the priest in charge that afternoon had recorded my words and presented me afterwards with a copy of the tape. Later, I discovered two women—one from Ireland, and the other from Scotland—had also asked for and received copies. Within less than a year, thousands of copies of the tape had been distributed all over Ireland and the United Kingdom, with the proceeds being used to bring clergy to Medjugorje. Heaven had done my promotional work for me: this tape, made without my knowledge, ended up paving the way for my mission far beyond the borders of the United States.

By the spring of 1988, I was well into the task of spreading the Medjugorje message. The road to conversion for the majority of those I encountered touched upon a need for reconciliation. So many lives had been shattered by divisions of one kind or another: marriages broken by divorce, children left without the security of family life, mainstream and non-denominational churches torn apart by petty disagreements and pride. Division was clearly Satan's tool of choice.

The mission was now international, allowing me to visit a country I had long admired and desired to see: Ireland. In an earlier tour there, I had been through just about every county, except for the six comprising Northern Ireland. On a second tour, this time in the north, I saw firsthand why Our Lady pleads so urgently for reconciliation among her children.

For hundreds of years, Catholics and Protestants have waged a murderous war against each other in Ireland. Many Americans think that all of Ireland is directly involved, but at the present time the conflict is limited to the six small counties of what is called Northern Ireland. Division arises from the fact that these counties, of a predominantly Protestant population, are legally part of the British Empire. That is an unacceptable sore point with the remaining Irish counties which are predominantly Catholic and politically independent of England. The Irish Catholics of Northern Ireland demand that all of Ireland be Irish, while the Irish Protestants of the six northern counties stubbornly cling to kinship with the British. That is the heart of the problem, though it can no longer be said that this alone fuels the violence and killing. Terrorism has become a self-sustaining evil feeding on a vicious circle of new atrocities and acts of vengeance.

In my first talk in Northern Ireland on the apparitions of Medjugorje, I asked how many there were Protestant. I did so because I had been told that many Protestants would come. Not one hand went up. Embarrassed, I wondered why I had even asked such a stupid question, and continued with the talk. I tried to place the message of Medjugorje into the hearts of all present, hoping to bring a ray of hope to a seemingly hopeless situation. I told my audience that Medjugorje's message is a message of love and peace, not war—especially war involving people who claim to be Christians.

After the talk, many approached me with a variety of comments and questions. I was shocked when one of them told me in a hushed, serious tone that there were many Protestants present at the talk but they did not reveal themselves out of fear. I further discovered that in daily life in Northern Ireland, Catholics and Protestants live and work together side by side. It is the militant, fanatical Catholic and Protestant groups formed into armies of hatred and identified by nationalistic names or initials, who continue the senseless slaughter.

In this talk and others on the tour, I related how I observed in Medjugorje Protestants and Catholics, Muslims and Jews, unbelievers and agnostics, skeptics and outright opponents, all arriving there on pilgrimage. I watched as they experienced dazzling conversion through the peace and love of the event as it unfolded for each of them. How wonderful it was to see those of the Jewish faith come to Medjugorje. Some convert to Christianity; others return home more devout in their Jewish faith. I have seen the same with Protestants, Muslims, and even non-believers who are renewed in peace and the desire to love and give service to others.

I told of the time several years ago when I took a Baptist minister and a Lutheran pastor to Medjugorje. Surprisingly, the Baptist minister had little difficulty accepting Mary's presence as messenger of God. The only difficulty, of course, was in the interpretation of Scripture from the Baptist perspective. He was able, however, to see the beauty and the goodness that was coming from Medjugorje. He was a direct witness to the good fruits of conversion to God.

On the other hand, the Lutheran pastor returned home completely confused and dismayed. He thought of Medjugorje only in ecumenical terms. For him, this was the coming together of the people of all faiths; for him, that meant sharing the sacraments, especially the Holy Eucharist. He soon realized that this was not the case, and spent the majority of the pilgrimage in his room in a state of despondency.

I attempted to explain to him that Medjugorje was not ecumenical per se; it was not Catholic or Baptist or Lutheran. It was, rather, a coming together of the children of God. A month after returning home, the Lutheran pastor suddenly discovered the real meaning of Medjugorje. Finally, the sense of peace and happiness he had seen in so many of his fellow pilgrims began to register. He is now a fervent witness to Medjugorje's good fruits.

I closed most of the talks in Northern Ireland by pointing out that in the face of ethnic and religious divisions, in the mire of distress of those lost in the darkness of sin, Our Lady of Medjugorje is saying to all of us: "You are my sons, you are my daughters!" She brings the same message to war-weary Northern Ireland.

I prayed that the people of Northern Ireland would be left with the thought that the message of Medjugorje is, above all things, a call for reconciliation for people of all faiths, all ethnic backgrounds, and all levels of society.

. . . . .

John said to him, "Teacher, we saw a man casting out demons in your name, and we forbade him, because he was not following us." But Jesus said, "Do not forbid him; for no one who does a mighty work in my name will be able soon after to speak evil of me."

Mark 9:38-39

Chapter 18

Live My Messages

A pilgrim crowd estimated at 100,000 filled the township of Medjugorje in celebration of the eighth year of daily apparitions. They listened with reverence, basking in the joy of being there on this special day in June 1989, as the Blessed Virgin gave this anniversary message: *Dear children, today I call you to live the messages which I have been giving you during the past eight years. This is a time of grace, and I desire the grace of God for every single one of you. I am blessing you and I love you with a special love. Thank you for your response to my call.*

Millions more throughout the world anxiously awaited the message. They had become followers of Medjugorje through these monthly messages which served to guide them along the same path of conversion as those fortunate enough to go there. Eight years of good fruits had brought the apparitions to this point. Now, every book, video and newsletter spawned by the phenomenon was eagerly received and passed on to family and friends.

Out of the spreading of the messages came a new way to "make a pilgrimage" to Medjugorje. A month before the eighth anniversary, the first national conference on Medjugorje was hosted by the University of Notre Dame. More than 5,000 followers of the apparitions came together to enjoy three days of retreat into holiness—very much akin to what takes place during pilgrimage at Medjugorje. Mass was celebrated, the rosary prayed, and witness given by those who had found the path of spiritual conversion through the apparitions.

I was blessed to be present for the Notre Dame conference as a last-minute inclusion on the guest speaker list. With a time slot of only fifteen minutes, I told my story. It would be the first of many Medjugorje conferences that would become a mainstay of speaking invitations for me.

Within two years, similar conferences were being held throughout the United States and in many other countries. The Franciscan priests stationed at the parish in Medjugorje, and the visionaries themselves, began coming as main attractions to bring their experiences to thousands who could not personally come to Medjugorje.

In August 1989, another Medjugorje phenomenon was launched: young people gathered there from all over the world for the first organized youth festival, as requested by the Blessed Mother. It purposely coincided with her special feast day, the Feast of the Assumption.

Late that night on Podbrdo Hill, she came in apparition for the second time that day as several thousand young people crowded together among the rocks and shrubbery. They were anxious to hear the words of the Virgin Mary, who gave this message to two of her visionaries: *My dear children, tonight, I am very, very, very happy!*

The visionaries later explained that they had "never seen Our Lady so radiantly happy!" The reason was simply that her appearances were working. People, especially young people, were responding. She asked that the Year of the Youth be extended into the coming years, adding that she would like to call it also the Year of the Family, with the festival as an annual event. There, in that message given to thousands of youth gathered in Medjugorje, was assurance that the Blessed Virgin would continue coming to Medjugorje at least through the next year.

This message came at an appropriate time: the local bishop had just issued an order to the Franciscan priests at Medjugorje forbidding the visionaries from going to the choir loft of Saint James Church for the daily apparitions. There was to be no more special apparition room within the church. No more priests were to be allowed to be present during the time of the apparition; no sick and handicapped pilgrims, and no media representatives. Panic set in among villagers and followers of Medjugorje. What would they do? Was this the end of the apparitions?

Such fears were soon put to rest as the apparitions continued. It seemed that, if only by the sheer number of consecutive appearances, heaven's plans would be accomplished in spite of the stumbling blocks raised by human beings. The Virgin continued to ask in her messages for the faithful to exert patience, understanding, and acceptance of such difficulties, even though they did not understand them; in other words, to live the messages in their daily lives with faith and trust, and perseverance.

But the Blessed Virgin is a kind and gentle mother. She does not ask us to bear up for too long! Eventually, she shows us why things "had" to happen the way they did. And so it was in this case, too. Soon I was to discover the meaning of the false obstacles created by the bishop.

In October of that same year I was back in Medjugorje. I stayed at visionary Marija's home, and was pleased that a mutual friend from Italy, Paolo Lunetti (who would later become Marija's husband) was also staying there. After greetings, Marija asked me to accompany Paolo to pick up her sister Ruska and her baby and bring them to Medjugorje from Ljbuski, a small town about twelve miles from Medjugorje. Marija was not feeling well, so her daily apparition would take place in her home that evening. She wanted her sister there for the apparition.

I must admit that, somewhat selfishly, I was happy Marija wasn't feeling all that well because it meant that her daily encounter with the Blessed Virgin Mary would take place there in the living room of her home, and I would be lucky enough to be present. I could hardly wait.

We brought Ruska and her six-month-old baby to the house. Shortly after, one of Marija's nieces, five-year-old Ivana, also came, followed a little later by one of her nephews, six-year-old Philip. Within minutes, there was the usual mass confusion created by little children at play. The apparition time was approaching and I began to wonder how we were going to have such a holy miracle take place in such a distracting setting. Marija hardly gave notice as she began to prepare.

Amidst the hustle and noise, her mother and father came into the room. A thought struck me. I asked Paolo if Marija's parents had ever been with her in the apparition room, and he told me they had not. Now, their faces were beaming because they were going to be there with their daughter as the Mother of Jesus came in apparition.

This was the setting: Marija, kneeling in front of a small statue in her tiny living room, began the rosary while the children continued running, laughing and playing. Ruska's baby was crying loud and long, while Marija's mother and father were praying with added fervor. Paolo and I were attempting to do the same. It went on this way until just moments before the apparition.

All at once, Marija motioned for Ivana and Philip to come and kneel beside her, one on each side. They suddenly became very quiet. The baby stopped crying almost as if on cue. There was instant peace and a sense of awe as Marija stopped her prayer in mid-sentence, and went into a state of ecstasy as the Blessed Virgin once again appeared to her.

I managed to glance at Marija's mother and father; the look on their faces was priceless. To see them so joyful was a joy in itself. In about two minutes, the apparition was over.

Immediately, the children returned to their games, and the baby was crying again. Marija, however, was beaming. She told us that the Blessed Virgin had come with three cherub angels, a practice that usually only occurs when she appears to the visionaries on Podbrdo Hill. The Blessed Mother looked at the little children in the room and said to Marija, *And you, also, have three angels with you!*

She then looked at each of us, Marija continued, and blessed us and then gave this message: *I wish for you to deeply live my messages I have given you.*

In that instant, all of the events of the past several months came together for me and I understood. The bishop had taken the apparitions out of the choir loft of the church, and indirectly placed them in the living rooms of the visionaries. Now, their families could be present for the apparitions. The Blessed Virgin had wanted us to make this the year of the family, to teach families to pray together and live the messages as a family, as well as individuals. This is where the praying of the rosary was to take primary importance; this was where fasting was to be done and where penance was to take place. There, in the home, with full family participation!

In an instant, in Marija's living room, I understood what the Blessed Virgin had been saying to us, and leading us to through the events of the past year. She desired that we first attempt to live the messages with our families; then, we would carry them over into our communities, work places, and schools.

I noticed during Mass at Saint James Church on the last night of our pilgrimage, that there were more local people there than I had seen in the last several trips. It was no special feast day or event. The people were simply there in the church centering on the Holy Eucharist and the beauty of the Mass. There was no apparition taking place in the choir loft, no flash bulbs popping, no one staring with hopes of seeing something supernatural. People were literally doing what the Medjugorje Madonna was asking and putting the spiritual first. In essence, we were being weaned away from the sensational and taught instead to rely on the spiritual.

Sitting on the side lawn for the final evening Mass of this latest trip, I watched people react in different ways. And, I found myself crying. I realized once again how the Virgin is pleading with us, sometimes with bitter tears, to live the messages. Sometimes, her tears are of blood because of the horrible sins of the world today. She cries, also, because of the controversy over the apparitions, and the lack of acceptance of them by church and laity, and the world in general.

The repetitious call in her messages was clear: We have to make them come alive in our lives so that we can hear once again that beautiful message from her as she spoke to the youth on Podbrdo Hill: *My dear children, today I am very, very, very happy!*

. . . . .

To him the gatekeeper opens; the sheep hear his voice, and he calls his own sheep by name and leads them out. When he has brought out all his own, he goes before them, and the sheep follow him, for they know his voice.   John 10:3-4

Chapter 19

Warning Signs

In September 1989, Mirjana became the second visionary to marry. She and her new husband, Marko Soldo, arrived in Portland, Oregon at the end of January 1990 to visit Father Milan Mikulic, who had performed their wedding ceremony in Medjugorje. This special priest, who was originally from the region, had asked her to visit his parish so that other priests and his bishop, a skeptic of the apparitions, would know of this great gift of heaven.

During this trip, the Blessed Virgin asked Mirjana by locution to prepare with prayer because she had a message for her. Mirjana entered the church and, as she started to pray, the Virgin again spoke to her by locution asking her to leave the church and go into the small chapel in the rectory. She gently reminded Mirjana that the bishop of Mostar, whose diocese included her home parish of Medjugorje, did not want her to have her apparitions in a church since he did not personally believe the apparitions were real.

It was a powerful lesson. The Mother of God was obeying a bishop's order, and telling her chosen visionary to do the same! Such obedience is a strong example of the testing of the spirit to assure that the encounters with the Blessed Virgin Mary at Medjugorje are from God. Without obedience, there is no real spirituality.

The message Mirjana received from the Virgin in apparition in the little chapel pointedly reflected the present dangerous state of the world, as well as the republics of the Federation of Yugoslavia. This is what the Madonna said: *I have been with you for nine years. For nine years, I wanted to tell you that God, your Father, is the only way, truth and life. I wish to show you the way to eternal life. I wish to be your tie, your connection to the profound faith. LISTEN TO ME! Take your rosary and get your children, your families with you. This is the way to come to salvation. Give your good example to your children; give a good example to those who do not believe. You will not have happiness on this earth, nei-*

102

ther will you come to heaven if you are not with pure and humble hearts and do not fulfill the law of God. I am asking for your help to join me to pray for those who do not believe. YOU ARE HELP- ING ME VERY LITTLE! You have little charity or love for your neighbor, and God gave you the love and showed you how you should forgive and love others. For that reason, RECONCILE and purify your soul. Take your rosary and pray it. All your suffering, take patiently. You should remember that Jesus was patiently suf- fering for you. Let me be your mother and your tie to God, to the Eternal Life. Do not impose your faith to the unbelievers. Show it to them by your example and pray for them. My children, PRAY! [emphasis added]

The Blessed Virgin's words to Mirjana in Portland brought into focus the essential spiritual elements of the Medjugorje messages. Its particularly urgent tone can be owed to the escalating division between ethnic groups in Yugoslavia at that time on the edge of outright war. Worse, pride and the desire for controlling power were splitting the Church of Bosnia-Hercegovina. The bishop of Mostar was still actively the strongest opponent of the appari- tions. Clearly, a frustrated mother was admonishing her children.

Could the people not see where the present path was leading? Had she not warned them in her second appearance to Marija on that first day of conversation with the visionaries, imploring them to reconcile their history of differences? How was it possible for the bishop and opposing priests not to see the good fruits of these nine years of supernatural guidance?

Even with such powerful intercession from the Blessed Virgin Mary, human hatred fed by centuries of division showed itself immune even to the supernatural. Even in the Church, the struggle for controlling power blinded those anointed to bring the Gospel message of Jesus to the flock. It seemed as if Satan was on the verge of upsetting all of heaven's plans by destroying the frame- work of peace forged in nine years of work by the Queen of Peace.

But true to the mercy of God, the apparitions continued. The Virgin's pleadings were only intensified, regardless of the refusal of so many people to listen, regardless of the blindness of the hierarchy of the local Church to the good fruits. The divine obedience shown by the Blessed Virgin in asking Mirjana to receive her in apparition in the small chapel rather than in the church only added to the unofficial authenticity of the phenomena. The bishop was still the bishop. No matter the motivation on his part, he was to be obeyed.

On the 25th of March, the Virgin gave her monthly message to Marija, stressing that she was still there for her children's salvation: *I am with you, even if you are not conscious of it. I want to protect you from everything that Satan offers you, and through which he wants to destroy you. As I bore Jesus in my womb, so also, dear children, do I want to bear you on to holiness. God wants to save you and send you messages through men, nature, and so many things which can only help you to understand; but you must change the direction in your life. Therefore, little children, understand also the greatness of the gift which God is giving you through me, so that I may protect you with my mantle and lead you to the joy of life.*

. . . . .

The year had begun in a war mode, with Iraq threatening to invade neighboring Kuwait. The world hung tensely on the edge of what could be the beginning of a globally destructive war.

In her first monthly message of the year (January 1989), the Blessed Virgin seemed to be addressing the situation directly: *Dear children, today, LIKE NEVER BEFORE, I invite you to prayer. Your prayer should be a prayer for peace. Satan is strong and wishes not only to destroy human life, but also nature and the planet on which we live. Therefore, dear children, pray that you can protect yourselves, through prayer, with the blessing of God's peace. God sends me to you so that I can help you if you wish to accept the rosary. Even the rosary alone can work miracles in the world and in your lives. I bless you and I stay among you as long as it is God's will. Thank you for not betraying my presence here, and I thank you because your response is serving God and peace.* [emphasis added]

In spite of the threat of retaliation from almost every oil-dependent nation in the world, tiny Kuwait was indeed invaded by Iraq. Now the gauntlet had been tossed on the ground, a line drawn and the dare to cross it given. Could this be the start of another world war? The people of the world held their breath as all-out invasion commenced to free oil-rich Kuwait. The call of free nations to defend against the invasion was successful. Kuwait was liberated and, within a week, peace was restored. Miraculously, global disaster was averted.

In Yugoslavia, however, threats turned into action and local clashes evolved into regional conflict. All-out war seemed a certainty. World leaders issued harsh condemnations and warnings to the Yugoslav leaders as sporadic clashes increased; but there was no mass reaction or international coalition of armies to guarantee justice and peace, as had been the case in Kuwait. Here, the control of oil interests was not at stake; the commodity was "only" human life and the right to freedom.

Unbelievably, the Western world, led by the United States, issued stern warnings that it would be "better" for the people economically if they stayed together in the Federation of Yugoslavia. Their motivation: to protect huge private investments in the economy of Yugoslavia, investments often controlled by men who had worked with the former Yugoslav regime. But were the people of this forced federation supposed to forget the years of brutal Communist rule, or their inherent desire to be free?

Abandoned by the free nations of the world, the countries of the former Yugoslavia marched steadily into armed conflict within their own borders. What could possibly turn back the tide of the violence to come?

In answer, the Virgin's March 18, 1991, annual message to Mirjana once again pointed to the only true solution: *Dear children, I am glad that you have gathered in such a large number. I would desire that you dedicate prayers for my children who do not know my love and the love of my Son. Help them to come to know it. Help me as Mother of all of you. My children, how many times I have already invited you here in Medjugorje to prayer and I will invite you again because I desire you to open your hearts to my Son, to allow Him to come in and fill you with peace and love. Allow Him, let Him enter! Help Him by your prayers in order that you might be able to spread peace and love to others, because that is now most necessary for you in this time of battle with Satan.*

The Virgin was identifying the real cause of the escalating conflict. She continued: *I have often spoken to you: pray, pray, because only by means of prayer will you drive off Satan and all the evil that goes along with Him. I promise you, my children, that I will pray for you, but I seek from you more vigorous prayers, and I seek you to spread peace and love which I am asking you in Medjugorje already nearly ten years. Help me, and I will pray to my Son for you.*

There was little doubt among believers that the Blessed Virgin was addressing the coming crisis. But again, the people did not listen, and an ugly wave of fanatical national pride ran roughshod over her words. On June 25, 1991—ironically, the tenth anniversary of the Medjugorje apparitions—Croatia announced its independence from the Federation of Yugoslavia, following the lead of Slovenia which had successfully done so months before.

Within hours, Croatia was in full military activity against insurgent Serbian forces aided by the "official" Yugoslav Army comprised of men and women from all of the republics of the Federation. What followed was a repetition of events in Slovenia, with one crucial difference. Slovenia, because of its distant northern geographical location, had escaped with little bloodshed and damage. Croatia would not be so fortunate.

Croatia's government leaders all but ignored the incredible miracle occurring in neighboring Bosnia-Hercegovina, even though it directly involved visionaries and villagers who were Croatian. Unprepared, armed only with national fervor and hunting rifles, the makeshift Croatian military plunged on in an attempt to break the bonds welded by years of Communist oppression, following headlong the stunning example of other Eastern European countries. Within weeks, the dream of independence became a nightmare: Croatia found itself in desperate need of essential supplies of food and medicine. Thousands were killed, and thousands more made homeless by the reality of active war.

On October 25, the Virgin gave the strongest of messages. She did not begin with her usual greeting of "Dear children," nor did she give her usual ending of "Thank you for having responded to my call." She only spoke three words, and she spoke them with great urgency: *PRAY! PRAY! PRAY!*

. . . . .

Too long have I had my dwelling place among those who hate peace. I am for peace; but when I speak, they are for war!

Psalms 120: 6-7

Chapter 20

Answering the Call

The threat of war engulfing Bosnia-Hercegovina meant facing a hard truth: pilgrimages to Medjugorje might soon be stopped by the danger. Even in the fall months of 1991, few pilgrimages were arriving, and those that did come were scant in numbers. Another hard truth had to be acknowledged: Medjugorje might never be the same. At least for the moment, the call to conversion through the phenomenon of the Blessed Virgin's apparitions had been effectively muted.

If pilgrims were unable to go to Medjugorje in the future, somehow, it seemed all right. Their absence would be sad, because the people of Medjugorje had become family for many who had traveled there; they had become brothers and sisters under the motherhood of Mary. But the essential element of the Blessed Virgin's appeal was for each pilgrim to live her messages. It was not enough just to read them, or say the rosary; it was not enough just attending church as often as possible. It wasn't even enough to make a pilgrimage to Medjugorje. The Blessed Virgin was constantly urging everyone who heard the messages to put them into practice in their actual, daily living.

For believers, the situation of war and the decline in pilgrimages meant an opportunity to discover the true nature of Medjugorje. If the messages live within us, then no one can bomb and destroy them. No one can take them away from us. Medjugorje is not just a village in Bosnia-Hercegovina where the Blessed Virgin Mary comes in daily apparition, but a way of fulfilling the call to holiness. It could easily be said that this is why Jesus had sent his Mother to the tiny village, to create in each heart an image of Medjugorje as a place of conversion to God.

This was the feeling of those intimately involved with Medjugorje. The threat of war would change nothing. They would continue to try and answer the Blessed Virgin's call, doing the best they could.

. . . . .

In August 1991, I arrived in Medjugorje leading a small pilgrimage including twelve teenage girls, most of whom were from my hometown of Myrtle Beach. We had an ominous arrival at a near-deserted airport just outside of Dubrovnik. Airplanes had been moved far away and flights were at a minimum in anticipation of armed conflict at any moment. Yugoslav military gunboats lay off the coast, in place and ready for attack. It was just a matter of timing.

I wondered again, as I had so often leading up to this trip, why we were coming at this time. Common sense dictated that it was not safe, especially for teenagers—most especially for teenage girls. But the pilgrims had insisted on coming—including the teenagers. Their parents wanted them to respond to the Blessed Virgin's call. Most disconcerting was the parents' conviction that everything would be all right because the young people were going with me. That only added to my anxiety.

In the setting of Medjugorje, it was hard to imagine the threat of war as close as the beautiful snow-capped mountains surrounding the little valley. Flare-ups had escalated to full battles throughout Croatia, and rumors of troops congregating in these hills and mountains for invasion of Bosnia had me on edge. Worse was talk of clashes in and around Dubrovnik—and at the airport. I prayed that we would be able to leave in a couple of days with no problems. Yet, once we arrived in the village, there was nothing but joy and a sense of safety and inner peace.

The following day, I was swamped with people asking questions and just wanting to talk. By the fourth evening of the pilgrimage, I desperately wanted to be alone, to simply be a pilgrim myself. I had not even climbed Podbrdo Hill, the original site of the apparitions. My time had been consumed from morning until evening giving talks and listening to stories of conversion.

On one particular evening, I went to the back of the church, where a large outdoor altar has been constructed. I sat down in the last row of seats away from everyone, satisfied to be alone at last. I noticed two men and two women sitting in the front row near the outside altar. One of the men was bent over, and at first, I thought he was crying. As I silently joined in the praying of the rosary coming over the outside loudspeakers, I could feel that familiar inner nudge of Our Lady; she was speaking to my heart, saying, *You should go and pray over him.*

I sat there and compromised, thinking, "I'll just say a prayer for him from here. It's the same thing." The minute I thought it, I knew it was wrong; but I rationalized that he was not feeling well and would not want a stranger to interfere. I continued to pray alone, adding a prayer for them.

Suddenly, there was a tap on my shoulder. I glanced up. Before me stood one of the women accompanying the sick man. She asked timidly, "I know people are always asking things of you, but I have a very special request. Could you please come and pray over that man up there in the front? Could you come say a prayer over him . . . ?" The young woman's voiced trailed off and she began to cry. "He's my brother and he is very sick. He has AIDS and he's dying. My mother and I brought him and his friend here hoping for a healing."

I felt horrible, knowing I had hesitated to do what the Blessed Virgin was asking. I had failed in this particular instance to answer the call. It was too late to pray over him at the time because of my hesitancy. There was no real prayer in me. Offering a weak apology, I asked if she would bring him back to the same place the next day, telling her I would be glad to pray over him at that time.

The following day, they came. Both men had AIDS. The man who was so sick was Catholic, while his partner, who had been living with him for seventeen years, was Protestant. The sick man was very repentant and open to what is happening in Medjugorje. He wanted a healing. The confused and frightened Protestant did not really understand what was going on. He knew nothing about Medjugorje or apparitions, but he was hoping this was all real, because they had no hope left.

We prayed together, all of us, and then I put my arms around both of them and prayed to Jesus that they both might be healed spiritually and physically.

I wouldn't have done that for anything in the world five years ago. I wouldn't have gotten near anyone with AIDS, let alone pray for their healing. I would have judged him in my heart and I would have condemned him. But the thought struck me. This was also war, the war of good against evil, the war that rages in all of us. It is in these situations that Our Lady primarily urges us to answer the call. Her messages center on the very words of Jesus when He says, "Whatever you do to the least of mine, you do to me." When we can see others as Jesus sees us and respond to them without judgment, then we can say we are answering the call.

· · · · ·

It was a wonderful pilgrimage. Everyone, including the teenagers, felt the same love, peace and happiness that others had felt before the threat of war.

The trip home wasn't easy. Arriving back in Dubrovnik, we found that our scheduled flight had been cancelled. Worse, there were no further flights for that day—or for the rest of the week. We were told that we would be put in a hotel near the Adriatic coast. Now I was deeply concerned. That particular location would be right in the line of fire of the expected attack on Dubrovnik. As the adults huddled together, trying to figure out just what to do, one of the young girls approached me with a suggestion: "Mr. Weible, we just came from Medjugorje and Our Lady tells us to pray and she'll take care of us. Why don't we do that?"

Out of the mouth of babes, I thought. Clearly, this young girl had heard the call. We immediately found a quiet corner and prayed the rosary. How Mary loves us, I thought! She continues to come to Medjugorje as the Queen of Peace and touch hearts, even into this stench of war. She comes to her children living there even though they are about to engage in horrible war.

Two hours later, after our travel agent had bargained with the Yugoslav airline officials, an aircraft was sent to transport us to Split, and then to Ljubliana, Slovenia, where finally we boarded a Lufthansa jet for Frankfort, Germany. We stayed over night there and found enough seats the following morning to return to the States.

I did not relax until I was sure each girl had been reunited with her family. For them, the intense situation in Dubrovnik and the extra day in Germany was exciting drama that only added to an already memory-packed trip. But the lessons and memories of prayer with these teenagers on the steps of St. James Church each evening would far outlast the excitement of the last day for all of us. They had heard the call.

Lying in my bed late into the night, I thanked Gospa again for the privilege of pilgrimage to Medjugorje—for the seventeenth time. Little did I realize it would be my last trip there for a long time to come.

. . . . .

There was again division among the Jews because of these words. Many of them said, "He has a demon, and he is mad; why listen to him?" Others said, "These are not the sayings of one who has a demon. Can a demon open the eyes of the blind?"

John 10:19-21

PART IV

Storm

For we are not contending against flesh and blood, but against the principalities, against the powers, against the world rulers of this present darkness, against the spiritual hosts of wickedness in the heavenly places.

Ephesians 6:12.

Chapter 21

Crisis

The Blessed Virgin spoke these words of peace and assurance in her January 1992 monthly message: *Dear children, today I am inviting you to renewal of prayer in your families, so that way, every family will become a joy to my Son, Jesus. Therefore, dear children, pray and seek more time for Jesus and then you will be able to understand and accept everything, even the most difficult sicknesses and crosses. I am with you and I desire to take you into my heart and protect you, but you have not yet decided. Therefore, dear children, I am seeking for you to pray, so through prayer you would allow me to help you. Pray, dear little children, so that prayer becomes your daily bread.*

She was addressing all of her children throughout the world, but was speaking most directly to the people of the former Yugoslav republics in the grip of an active war. The conflict would soon include Bosnia-Hercegovina.

With the people in extreme anxiety and stress, the very fact of her continuing apparitions was reassurance that in spite of human failure, she remained faithful. Sporadic rays of hope would break through as negotiations took place between the warring factions. Truces were signed with the hope of putting an end to the fighting and destruction. Some of the negotiations and resulting truces were conducted in Medjugorje, now recognized by all involved as a place of special peace. By January 1992, fifteen such truces had been broken.

On the exterior, life seemed normal enough under the conditions. Pilgrimages still arrived, though group numbers were reduced to a fraction of what they were prior to the hostilities. Still, the people came, in spite of the circumstances. They came for the same reasons as pilgrims before them, but with an added mission: to help the war victims in response to the Virgin's plea.

Locally, some good did evolve from an obviously bad situation: many "outsiders" who had come only to exploit the apparitions for profit began to flee the area. Construction of restaurants, hotels, and souvenir shops was abruptly halted. The village underwent a much-needed cleansing from activities that had threatened to overwhelm the holiness wrought by the apparitions. It soon involuntarily returned to the quiet, uneventful life of pre-apparition days.

While this return to a calmer life was a welcome change, in reality, it was the quiet before the storm.

In February, the Blessed Virgin gave this message: *Today, I invite you to draw still closer to God through prayer. Only that way will I be able to help you and to protect you from every attack of Satan. I am with you and I intercede for you with God that He protect you, but I need your prayers and your yes. You get lost easily in material and human things and forget that God is your greatest friend. Therefore, my dear little children, draw close to God so that He may protect you and guard you from every evil.*

In Mirjana's annual apparition on March 18, the Blessed Virgin followed with this urgent warning: *I need your prayers, now, more than ever before! I beseech you to take your rosary in your hands, now, more than ever before. Grasp it strongly, and pray with all your heart in these difficult times.*

Less than a month later, April 6, Bosnia-Hercegovina was under attack. The insurgent Bosnian Serbs, bolstered by the Federal Army of Yugoslavia, attacked with fury. Women and children began to flee. Churches, monasteries, convents, schools, hospitals, and historic sites became prime targets. They were the first to be mercilessly destroyed. Only seventeen miles from Medjugorje, the city of Mostar was under constant shelling. The Cathedral was critically damaged, while the bishop's residence and offices were bombed and burned. Bombs fell on Citluk, only three miles from Medjugorje. For the first time in its history, Saint James Church was closed, boarded, and without Holy Mass. Priests, nuns, villagers, and a straggling of pilgrims huddled in the basement of the rectory for services and protection.

But the "Woman Full of Grace" was still there, still appearing to the visionaries. She continued to intercede and plead for prayers and fasting to end the fighting.

In early May, bombs were dropped on Medjugorje; they did little or no damage, many exploding high above the village or falling into the surrounding fields without detonating. Two Russian-made MIG fighter jets were sent to destroy the village, especially Saint James Church. They came on a clear, cloudless morning, but as they approached their target, suddenly the valley was covered in dense clouds and they could not see to drop their bombs. One plane was downed while the other returned to its base. The surviving pilot, filled with superstitious fear and only a flicker of faith, defected from his military unit, knowing he had witnessed a miracle.

News of the war surrounding Medjugorje traveled quickly around the world. A huge network had developed without specific design, using telephone, fax, and Internet technologies. It hummed with activity as news arrived. Prayer groups prayed with added intensity, attempting to comply with the Virgin's urgent plea. Tour companies wondered what would happen to planned pilgrimages. Former pilgrims worried about Bosnian families and individuals whom they had befriended during past pilgrimages.

. . . . .

On the home front, I continued with my speaking engagements. All planned trips to Medjugorje, however, were cancelled. Although I had averaged two or three trips per year, I could not justify going into an active war zone. Every article or television report on the crisis brought mixed feelings. I recoiled from the thought of danger, but at the same time I wanted to be there with the people who had become like family. Especially, I wanted to be with the visionaries and priests. All I could really do was pray and fast for a swift end to the hostilities.

The questions asked at the talks now centered primarily on the war. What was happening in the village? Was it under attack? Were the visionaries okay? But the most frequently asked question was this: How could war occur in a place where heaven had sent the Blessed Virgin Mary to speak directly to mankind? It was difficult for the believer to comprehend, much less for the skeptic.

Yet, the answer was clear: this was the age-old battle between good and evil, between the principalities and the powers. For us, the choice was there for the making: follow God, or follow Satan. The Blessed Virgin had given the warning in the first days, pointing out the necessity of reconciliation. In every apparition she *asked*, or *invited*, or *pleaded* with us to live the messages, never demanding or ordering us to do so, thanking us for the times we responded.

I spoke frequently of the village in the beginning days of the apparitions, telling audiences how it had been so spiritually pristine. That was the best way I could describe it. It had been a place of holy exuberance, the edge of heaven, and like so many that had made pilgrimage there, I felt I could have stayed forever. I pointed out that in the following years, the pristine atmosphere slowly began to thin; pilgrimages were watered down with the curious and those who came strictly as tourists. Travel agencies, anxious to cash in, planned side trips for shopping or sightseeing in other parts of the country, taking pilgrims away from pilgrimage. The presence of the Virgin each evening became almost commonplace for many villagers who seemed to have forgotten the wonder and enthusiasm of the first days.

But all this was to be expected; in fact, if everything had been perfect from the early days to the present, the authenticity of the apparitions would have been suspect. For those who understand the real nature of the battle, the human pollution surrounding such an overwhelming supernatural event was no real surprise. Still, it was disappointing. Many pilgrims who had experienced life-changing conversion through Medjugorje were now busy traipsing after every purported visionary and locutionist. They seemed driven with an insatiable thirst to know every possible detail about any supernatural event. The monthly message given to visionary Marija was now awaited more out of curiosity than a desire to welcome it and make it part of daily life.

Sadly, I related, Medjugorje became a place of material opportunity for many. New entrepreneurs came in droves. They arrived as rapacious wolves disguised as converted sheep, attempting to cash in quickly on the desires of those in search of miracles. Cafes and souvenir stands sprung up almost over night, along with hotels, barracks, and constant construction as villagers continued to build additional rooms onto their homes to house pilgrims. Many villagers who had responded so fervently in the beginning months of the apparitions were now too busy making money like they had never made it before. They were too busy to attend evening Mass, too occupied with newfound money-making opportunities to pray a family rosary, or to fast on Wednesday and Friday as requested by the Virgin.

Each year brought greater gifts from heaven; at the same time, with the addition of each new business, new room, and new souvenir shop, it was as if Satan was delivering blow after blow to the spiritual body of Medjugorje. And then, I pointed out to the audiences, the greatest blow: war—bloody, pain-filled, havoc-wreaking, killing war—the total "unpeace" of Satan.

After ten years, pilgrimage to the village was effectively stopped; only the die-hards dared to venture into what was now a war-ravaged countryside. Bombs fell on and around Medjugorje, but somehow they did little or no damage to the church, the hill where the Blessed Virgin had first appeared, or to Cross Mountain. Yet, homes and businesses on the road leading to Medjugorje were damaged or destroyed, as were other entire villages in the area. Regardless of its seeming immunity from the devastation of war, for all intents and purposes, Medjugorje was shut down. It appeared that Satan had won.

One question lay on the hearts of everyone: Could Medjugorje survive the war? Not just the physical Medjugorje, but the spiritual Medjugorje. Would it continue to give spiritual nourishment to a world starved for authentic love and peace? I told my audiences that the answer depended entirely on whether or not believers responded to the call that had been sounded by the Blessed Virgin for nearly eleven years.

Bluntly, I repeated over and over, it was a time for a new commitment. Here, I related, is how the Virgin put it in her March 25, 1992, monthly message to the followers of Medjugorje: Dear children, today as never before, I invite you to live my messages and to put them into practice in your life. *I have come to you to help you, and therefore, I invite you to change your life because you have taken a path of misery, a path of ruin. When I told you 'Convert, pray, fast, and be reconciled,'* **you took these messages superficially.** *You started to live them and then you stopped because it was difficult for you.* [emphasis added]

Know, dear children, when something is good, you have to persevere in the good and not think, 'God does not see me, He is not listening, He is not helping.' And so, you have gone away from God and from me because of your miserable interests. I wanted to create of you an oasis of peace, love, and goodness. God wanted you, with your love and His help, to do miracles and thus give an example.

Therefore, here is what I say to you: *Satan is playing with you, and with your souls, and I cannot help you because you are far from my heart. Therefore, pray, live my messages and then you will see the miracles of God's love in your everyday life. Thank you for responding to my call.* [emphasis added]

As always, I told audiences that the Blessed Virgin had the answer. She gave it again in her April 25th monthly message: *Today also I invite you for prayer. Only by prayer and fasting can war be stopped. Therefore, my dear little children, pray, and by your life give witness that you are mine and that you belong to me, because Satan wishes in these turbulent days to seduce as many souls as possible.* [emphasis added]

Therefore, I invite you to decide for God and He will protect you and show you what you should do and which path to take. I invite all those who have said yes to me to renew their consecration to my Son, Jesus, and to His heart and to me so we can take you more intensely as instruments of peace in this unpeaceful world. Medjugorje is a sign to all of you and a call to pray and live the days of grace that God is giving you. Therefore, little children, accept the call to prayer with seriousness. I am with you, and your suffering is also mine.

The Virgin's plan was a plan of peace, a plan that would have prevented all of the horror if only the people had listened. As visionary Vicka was quoted as saying, "The Blessed Mother said that she could stop this war easily if only we would pray and fast . . ."

．．．．．

What causes wars, and what causes fighting among you? Is it not your passions that are at war in your members? You desire and do not have; so you kill. And you covet and cannot obtain; so you fight and wage war. You do not have, because you do not ask. You ask and do not receive, because you ask wrongly, to spend it on your passions. James 4: 1-3

Chapter 22

Dark Fruits of the Battle

Sitting quietly in the cramped aisle seat of the airplane, I wondered what I was doing returning to Medjugorje. The war was raging. One could hardly imagine the horrors being done by humans to other humans. Suddenly, the thought struck me. It was January 25, 1993, the anniversary day of the apparitions, and the day the Blessed Virgin Mary gave her monthly message to the world through visionary Marija.

Just as suddenly, I knew why I was returning; there was a two-fold purpose. First, it was necessary to see firsthand the effects of the war. Father Svetozar Kraljevic, a Franciscan priest involved with the apparitions as a spiritual advisor to the visionaries, and now a close personal friend, urged me to come. Quietly and without drama, he pointed out that I did not know the Medjugorje of the war years. I had not seen firsthand how Satan's plan of attack was attempting to change the face of Medjugorje. How could I speak of this miracle, its messages and the conversions occurring even in the depths of evil's reign, if I did not come and see for myself?

Thus, after an absence of eighteen months, I arrived in the country that had become like a second home. Father Svetozar was at the airport in Split to greet me and drive us to Medjugorje. We stopped briefly to deliver a cash donation to a priest who coordinated relief efforts in the region. It felt especially good to give it to this priest personally, knowing it would go directly to assist the most destitute. There were so many hungry and homeless families and individuals without hope, he told us, with precious little time to wait on slow-moving government agencies and charitable organizations.

As we drove, Father Svetozar spoke of similar relief efforts taking place throughout the region. Remarkably, millions of dollars in donations, food, and medicine were pouring in from many different countries. The sources were Medjugorje-based prayer groups and newly-formed organizations operated by people who had previously come to Medjugorje on pilgrimage. Now, they were returning to help the war victims, in direct response to the Blessed Virgin's frequent requests for penance. They were ordinary people—housewives, businessmen and students—risking their lives to enter into active battle zones to help others.

As we drove the dangerous roads in what seemed the darkest of nights, the reality of war struck home. Frequent stops at heavily armed checkpoints, together with many detours created by unsafe conditions due to active fighting, delayed our arrival into Medjugorje until the early morning hours.

Once there, I noted how the atmosphere was as different as light is from darkness. There was an immediate feeling of peace, a sense of security and safety, of being "home" again. I was thankful to Father Svetozar for convincing me to come and see that, in spite of the horror of war, the grace of Medjugorje continued.

There were noticeable differences. The following morning, I arrived at Saint James Church for the English-speaking Mass only to find it empty. On inquiring if there was to be an English Mass that morning, I was directed to the small room on the right side of the altar that had once served as the site of the apparitions. Inside was a small band of pilgrims, mostly Italians and a few Americans. Despite the cramped quarters and diminished crowd, the holiness of Mass in Medjugorje was the same. It was just as awe-inspiring as when thousands filled and surrounded the church before the war.

Afterwards, I found a copy of the January 25, 1993, monthly message on the church bulletin board: *Dear children, today I call you to accept and live my messages with seriousness. These days are the days when you need to decide for God, for peace and for the good. May every hatred and jealousy disappear from your life and your thoughts, and may there only dwell love for God and for your neighbor. Thus, only thus, shall you be able to discern the signs of this time. I am with you and I guide you into a new time, a time which God gives you as grace, so that you may get to know Him more. Thank you for having responded to my call.*

Reading it several times, I knew the second reason for my return to Medjugorje. It was not just to see the results of the war, but to once again be a pilgrim. I wanted to climb Cross Mountain, and Podbrdo Hill where the Blessed Virgin Mary had first appeared. I wanted to sit in the church for long periods of time and pray, just to be in the presence of God.

But first, there was work to do. Father Svetozar was to drive me into the city of Mostar for an up-close look at the dark fruits of war. It had to be now since he was leaving in two days to attend to more fund raising for relief efforts. Waves of anxiety and fear were intermingled with a gauntlet of emotions as we cautiously made our way along the bomb-scarred road into the city.

The war scenes were far worse than what I had seen in pictures. Mostar was a mess, suffering devastation as severe as reported in Sarajevo. It seemed, Father Svetozar told me, that every time repairs were started, the shelling would be renewed. Serb forces hunkered in the surrounding mountains lobbed shells daily into population centers, shopping areas, churches and hospitals. As I stared at a crater-sized hole in the side of a new hospital building, I realized that the entire scene would forever be etched in my mind. The former hospital administrator, a Serbian, was now in the hills assisting in the shelling of the hospital and its clinic.

I stopped taking notes and just looked at the destruction of what had once been a thriving city and tourist attraction. Parks were now cemeteries. Mounds of rubble rose where apartments used to stand. Hotels were command posts and headquarters for the media. There was no need to record detail. This was, as in all wars, the terrible fruit that comes without the true peace of God. The opening words of the January monthly message came to mind: *Dear children, today I call you to accept and live my messages with seriousness* . . . This was the result of not taking the messages seriously, of not praying and fasting, or attempting to reconcile. The hatred and jealousy of misguided, ethnic pride had shut out the love of God.

Back in Medjugorje, I did finally manage to climb Podbrdo, scurrying up the small hill just a half-hour before leaving for Split and the return flight home. There was time for only a few minutes of prayer—a few very intense minutes of prayer. Everything I had experienced in the past seventeen trips to Medjugorje seemed to flash before me. I was humbly grateful that the Virgin Mary had prompted me to return, not just to witness the darkness of war, but for these precious moments at the very spot where she had first appeared to the children. I thanked her for the reminder that only through prayer, fasting and penance would the war come to an end.

. . . . .

A month later, having completed a speaking tour in Italy, I was with visionary Marija and her fiancé Paolo Lunetti at his parents' home in Monza, Italy, when she received the February 25, 1993, monthly message. This was one of several occasions that I witnessed Marija receiving the monthly message. Each time reaffirmed for me the incomprehensible grace being poured out to the world through the apparitions.

We began the rosary and prayed the first four decades. Marija then knelt in front of a small statue of the Blessed Virgin Mary. After several more minutes of prayer, the Virgin came in great peace and stayed for about four minutes, giving Marija the message. I could feel an indescribable love as she blessed us before leaving in a cross of light. Marija stated afterwards that Our Lady was very quiet and peaceful during the apparition.

Father Slavko Barbaric, Marija's spiritual director, telephoned from Medjugorje just past six o'clock to receive and record the message. It would then be carefully scrutinized for scriptural and doctrinal compliance, before being translated into numerous languages for worldwide distribution. After so many years, this had become the procedure.

Here is the message that was given to Marija that day: Today I bless you with my motherly blessing and I invite you all to conversion. *I desire each of you to decide for change in your life and that you work more in the church, not with words, not with thoughts, but with your example. Let your life be a joyful witness of Jesus. You cannot say you are converted because your life must become an every day conversion. To understand what you have to do, little children, pray, and God will give you to know what you*

have to do concretely and where you need to change. I am with
you and keep you always under my mantle.

A month later (March), she gave this message: *Today, like
never before, I call you to pray for peace: for peace in your
hearts, peace in your families, and peace in the whole world,
because Satan wants war . . . wants lack of peace . . . wants to
destroy all which is good. Therefore, dear children, PRAY! PRAY!
PRAY!* [emphasis added]

Remarkably, even with the war at its zenith, the good fruit of
the miracle of Medjugorje continued to come forth. The village
itself remained a cool spot in the middle of an inferno. Less than
twelve miles away, a defensive front was established and the war
raged. Men from the village would go for short periods of time to
join in the defense of their country before returning to local jobs
and family. Buses carrying them to the front lines would stop in
front of Saint James Church where the men would pray a decade
of the rosary. Almost every soldier wore a rosary around his neck.
In July, the first soldier from Medjugorje was killed in action.

The visionaries carried on with the task of spreading the messages. Marija had just returned from a speaking tour in Brazil. She
was never comfortable speaking in front of crowds, not even in
Medjugorje when pilgrims came to her home. Now, she had
toured Brazil, speaking in front of thousands. In obedient humility, she had accepted this personal penance in direct answer to the
Blessed Virgin's plea to witness to the messages.

Plans had also been announced for Marija's wedding to Paolo
Lunetti in September, giving cause for concern among the Franciscans of Medjugorje. Would this disrupt the flow of monthly
messages, or the pattern of the apparitions, especially since Marija would be living in Monza, Italy? Marija assured them that she
and her husband would be visiting the village frequently, and that
nothing concerning her part in the daily appearances of the Virgin
would change, as far as she knew. However, concern remained.
The other visionaries who had married had settled in the village.
She would be the first one to be living outside of the direct spiritual guidance of the Franciscans.

Ivan was touring in Australia, witnessing before thousands and doing an excellent job. The shy young man now confidently spoke about family values and prayer, stressing the need for young people to find the path of spiritual conversion.

Even Jakov, always reluctant to be on public display, was in Italy giving talks. In April, he would also marry, his bride a beautiful Italian girl whom he met when she came to Medjugorje on pilgrimage. They would settle in the village and eventually begin taking pilgrims into their home.

Meanwhile, Vicka remained in Medjugorje doing what she had done so well for eleven-plus years: serving as unofficial ambassador to the few remaining pilgrims coming to Medjugorje. How many times had I seen huge crowds in and around her modest home to hear her story and have her pray over the sick. On this recent trip, I passed by her home one day and observed her giving a talk to only two pilgrims. The enthusiasm was the same as when the crowds were in the hundreds.

．　．　．　．　．

June 25, 1993, marked the twelfth anniversary of the apparitions and, incredibly, nearly 30,000 pilgrims were present. The crowd included approximately four thousand people from the United States, and literally thousands from Slovenia, Croatia, and Bosnia-Hercegovina. It was an incredible display of faith that so many would travel into an active war zone; it was a pure response of love and belief.

And, in response to the huge turnout, the Blessed Virgin gave this anniversary message: *Dear children, today also I rejoice at your presence here. I bless you with my motherly blessing and I intercede for each one of you before God. I call you anew to live my messages and to put them into life and practice. I am with you and bless all of you day by day. Dear children, these times are special and, therefore, I am with you to love and protect you, to protect your heart from Satan and to bring you all closer to the heart of my Son, Jesus. Thank you for having responded to my call.*

Even in the midst of battle, she came to plead, warn and reassure.

．　．　．　．　．

127

For you were called to freedom, brethren; only do not use your freedom as an opportunity for the flesh, but through love be servants of one another. For the whole law is fulfilled in one word, "You shall love your neighbor as yourself." But if you bite and devour one another take heed that you are not consumed by one another. Galatians 5:13-15

Chapter 23

Martyr

Not all of the people traveling to Medjugorje went as pilgrims in the pure sense of the word. Collette Webster, for example, did not join an organized pilgrimage; in fact, she did not even know about the apparitions of the Blessed Virgin Mary taking place in the little village, or of their global impact. This young woman didn't go seeking answers to troubling spiritual questions or looking for direction in life. Instead, the twenty-seven-year-old American from Michigan traveled to Medjugorje in January 1993 on a personal mission to aid the victims of the war in Bosnia-Hercegovina. She went there especially to help the children.

Nine months later, Collette Webster, having no special ties to the cause or its people, was killed by a sniper in the city of Mostar, moments after tending the critical wounds of a Croatian soldier. She saved his life and lost her own. She gave the greatest of gifts and fulfilled all that is asked by the Blessed Virgin Mary through her apparitions in Medjugorje.

In return, Collette received heaven's greatest distinction: she became a martyr.

Her mission began at home in the little town of Sunfield, when Collette met and befriended a high school exchange student from Sarajevo. The young girl had been sent to the States by her parents to escape the dangers of the war. As she spoke of the horrors taking place in Bosnia-Hercegovina, something clicked inside of Collette; she just knew she was supposed to go and do what she could to help. Without a second thought, plans and preparations commenced for the mission of her life.

Never too well organized in the past, Collette uncharacteristically immersed herself in a study of the area, its history of struggle, and the current situation. She carefully read newspaper and magazine articles about the war, learning all she could. To prepare herself for her mission, she enrolled in an emergency medical training course at a nearby fire department.

Shortly thereafter, in September 1992, Collette told her father she intended to get rid of everything she owned and go to Bosnia to become a relief worker for the war victims. He was shocked. But not too shocked. John Webster's oldest daughter had always been different. She was infamous for spur-of-the-moment actions, reflected later in adult life as she jumped from job to job, drove too fast, and was involved in countless accidents. She ate poorly, chain-smoked, and suffered from asthma and insomnia; and, she seemingly never stopped moving.

Personal relationships followed the same helter-skelter course, resulting in an ill-advised marriage to an older man already twice divorced. Predictably, it ended the same way, though on amiable terms. It was the only way Collette knew how to handle relationships. She had no enemies.

Having made the decision to go, Collette gave her car to her sister, sold most of her possessions, and signed over to her soon-to-be former husband full ownership of an old house they had purchased with the intent of renovating it themselves. It was another in an endless list of things planned but never accomplished. She also gave him outright ownership to a failing convenience store business they had started, the pressure of its operation being a decisive blow to their marriage.

Such generosity under these conditions might be viewed as foolish or impetuous, but it simply highlighted another strong characteristic of Collette. Always sensitive and caring, she had a heart as big as they come. Animals, people, charitable causes—anyone or anything she could love, she did.

In answer to her father's query of why this cause, why this country, Collette replied without hesitation: "Everybody sits and talks about problems, and nobody ever does anything. I just can't watch this happen . . ." Before she left, she gave him a bookmark that read: "You never know until you try."

Resigned to her decision, Collette's family saw her off on her first-ever venture outside of the United States. She departed in

January 1993, with a thousand dollars cash, a suitcase full of donated medicines, and a large duffel bag packed with food and clothes. Within weeks, part of her money had been stolen, and she had given refugees her wool socks and one of her two pairs of boots. She lived in a small room in Medjugorje, soon shared with four other relief workers.

Hardship aside, Collette discovered the pure joy of giving as never before. A stranger had told her on the plane to Zagreb to go to Medjugorje. There, he told her, she would find plenty of work helping war victims. The stranger was right; within days of arriving in Medjugorje, Collette was fully involved in relief work.

She also discovered the miracle of the apparitions of the Blessed Virgin Mary, rekindling a weak flame of faith that had long been dormant. Collette had been raised Catholic and knew a little about the faith, but had lost contact with God and His Church. Her parents divorced and remarried, going their separate ways. Over time, Collette's formal but infrequent church affiliation eventually settled at a Protestant church.

In Medjugorje, Collette was soon immersed in work at nearby refugee camps, orphanages, and hospitals. She became hardened to the constant thunder of guns and the gory realism of applying medical skills learned on-the-job—even assisting on one occasion at an amputation.

Yet, even in the midst of such daily horrors, the people of Bosnia captured Collette's heart, especially the children. It didn't matter whether they were Christian or Muslim. For her, there was no good or bad here, no political affiliation in this tragedy; there were just victims. She didn't care which side they were on. Collette simply had to hug every child she saw. Without being conscious of it, she was living the Medjugorje message.

Noticeably changed, the young American volunteer returned home for a brief visit in June, staying just long enough to celebrate her twenty-seventh birthday and plead for finances to help the relief cause. She had been slightly wounded by a bullet flying through her hair as she assisted others to safety. A relieved family, thankful to have her home, saw other differences.

Unpredictable, impetuous Collette now had serenity, inter-mixed with fervent zeal for humanitarian service. She talked of going other places where she might be needed when this conflict ended. Her family had never seen her so focused—or so anxious to return to her mission. Around her neck on a handmade neck-lace, she wore a plastic baby's pacifier, along with two bullet cas-ings, given to her by a little refugee girl. It was a perfect symbol of the struggle of which she was now a part.

News of Collette's involvement spread, and soon newspapers and other media were calling for interviews. When asked why she was involved in a conflict where she had no personal affiliation, she replied, "I don't really know why. I'm Irish, I have no rela-tionship to these people, but I've always been the type of person who stood up for the underdog."

Collette talked about the war, telling of shells exploding near and around her and other workers. She quietly told of refugees who saw relatives raped, tortured, killed and hanged; victims of atrocities beyond imagination or description. "You know it's hap-pened," she said in one interview, "because you read about it, but when you meet someone who it's happened to, you still can't fully understand that person's plight unless you've been through it."

Filled with emotion, she spoke of little children coming into the refugee centers so shaken and suffering from shock that they attacked everyone around them that was a stranger. "Kids seem to adapt easier than anybody," she said, "but they also seem to suf-fer the most long-term effects." Her joy, she added, was when these little ones could hug again.

Yet, she couldn't wait to return. Her next trip home would be for Christmas she assured her family. But Collette would never return home again.

Frustrated in the ensuing months because of the lack of aid and finances, Collette took the final step in her mission. In early Sep-tember, she joined the Croatian Army as a front-line medic so she could do more. On Sunday, September 26, approximately a year from the time she first told her father of her plans to go to Bosnia, she entered the final moments of her mission.

The day had started on a happy note. Collette and several friends delivered a just-baked apple pie to some soldiers on duty in Mostar. Later, she and the other volunteers entered a bombed-out building in an area notorious for fierce fighting. She found a young Croatian soldier near death from severe wounds. As Collette dressed the soldier's injuries, she was warned to stay low because snipers were active across the street from the building.

Finishing her task, she stood up without thinking, suddenly silhouetted in a nearby window. It was a foolish, impulsive action. Her army uniform became an inviting target, making her just another of the enemy to the unknown sniper. Suddenly, a loud boom and a flash of light. Shrapnel ripped through her stomach. Collette slumped to the cluttered floor, her intestines exposed. As she looked at her wound, she calmly told her companions, "I'm not going to live," adding moments later, "Tell my sister I love her."

Collette died several hours later on the operating table of the hospital where she had so many times assisted other war victims. Her time in Medjugorje had not been spent climbing the hill where the apparitions first occurred, or scaling Cross Mountain. She did not spend every evening in Saint James Church at Mass, or join very often in the prayers of the rosary during her days in the village.

Collette was too busy living the message. She paid the ultimate price and received the ultimate reward of martyrdom.

· · · · ·

Greater love has no man than this, that a man lay down his life for his friends.   John 15:13

Chapter 24

What Then Is My Suffering?

War is the full presence of Satan and the total absence of God. Satan always comes where the Blessed Virgin Mary is sent to bring God's peace. He comes to destroy that peace. He came to Bosnia-Hercegovina with the sole intent of destroying the fountain of grace pouring forth from the tiny village of Medjugorje. Neither ethnic differences nor opposing religions caused this abyss of darkness; they were just the tools. Like all wars, this conflict grew from the hell-inspired contest of greed and power and pride, another chapter in an endless story.

Yet, God creates light where there is only darkness. He brings forth good seed from utter desolation and hopelessness. It is the seed of the harvest.

Here, in this bitter account, is a graphic illustration of the horror of the war that ravaged Bosnia-Hercegovina. It is written by a young woman, at that time a devoted religious, who had suffered the outrage of rape and its fruit of shame. Her story reveals Satan's bitter hatred of God's chosen ones, the women who have consecrated their lives to Him as nuns.

The story is told in the words of the woman herself, by way of a letter written to the superior of her convent. It is edited only for clarity and to protect the identity of the nun and her order. It states all that is necessary to describe the full inhumanity of this war. At the same time, it is an incomprehensible response that can only come through total conversion to God.

It is the perfect response to Medjugorje's message:

Dear Mother,

I am one of the novices who were raped by the militant Serbs. I am writing to you in regard to what happened to my sisters and me.

Permit me not to give you any details. It was an atrocious experience, incommunicable except to God, under whose Will I placed myself during my consecration to Him as I made my vows. My tragedy is not only the humiliation I was subjected to as a woman, or the irreparable offense against my choice of existence and to my vocation, but the difficulty of inscribing deep in my faith, an event which is certainly part of the mysterious Will of the One I still consider to be my Divine Spouse.

Only a few days before, I had read a dialogue of the Carmelites of Bernanos, and the thought had come to me to ask our Lord to let me die a martyr. He took me at my word.

I find myself today in an obscure interior anguish. They have destroyed my life's plan, which I had considered permanent; now, they have traced another, which I have not yet succeeded in unraveling. In my teens, I had written in my private diary: "Nothing is mine; I belong to no one and no one belongs to me." Yet, one night, which I do not want to remember, someone took me and wrested me from myself and made me his.

When I came to, it was daylight. My first thought was of our Lord's agony in the Garden of Olives. A terrible struggle took place within me. On one hand, I asked myself, why did God allow me to be broken to pieces and destroyed precisely where I had placed my reason for living. And, to what new vocation was He leading me on this new path?

I got up, exhausted, while I helped one of my sisters, and then I got dressed. I heard the bell ring at the

Monastery next to ours. I made the sign of the cross and mentally recited the liturgical hymn: "At this hour, on Golgotha, the True Pascal Lamb, Christ, pays the ransom for our sins to redeem us."

What then, Mother, is my suffering and the offense endured, in comparison to that of the One to whom I promised a thousand times to give my life? I said slowly, "Your Will be done, especially now that I have no other support but the certainty that You, Lord, are at my side."

I write to you, Mother, not to seek your consolation, but your help in giving thanks to God for letting me join millions of compatriots, offended in their honor, and to accept this maternity not wished for. My humiliation is added to that of the others. I can only offer it in expiation for the sins committed by the unknown rapists, and for peace between two opposed ethnic groups, by accepting the dishonor I endure and then offer to God's mercy.

Do not hold it against me if I ask you to share with me a "grace" which may seem absurd. These past months, I shed all my tears for my two brothers, assassinated by the very ones who terrorize and attack our towns. I did not think my suffering could be worse, or that the pain could reach any greater dimension.

Every day, hundreds of scrawny-looking people, trembling with cold and bearing a look of despair, knock on the door of our convents. A few weeks ago, a young girl of eighteen told me: "You do not know what dishonor is."

I thought hard about what she said and knew that it was a question of my people in pain, and I was almost ashamed of living close to all this suffering. Now, I am one of them. One of my people's many anonymous women whose body is torn to bits and whose soul is ransacked. The Lord has made me penetrate into the mystery of this shame, and also to the religious that I am. He has accorded me the privilege of understanding the diabolical force of evil.

I know that from now on, the words of courage and consolation I will try to speak from my poor heart will be believed, because my story is their story; my resignation, strengthened by faith, will be, if not an example, of some help to confront their moral and emotional reactions. God has chosen me—may He forgive the presumption—to guide these humiliated people toward a dawn of redemption and freedom. They will not doubt the sincerity of my intentions since, like them, I too come from the frontier of abjectness.

I remember that during my studies in Rome, a Slavic professor of literature had read to me this verse by Alesej Mislovic: "You must not die, because you were chosen to be on the side of light." On the night I was raped by the Serbs, I repeated this verse which was like balm on my soul when despair threatened to destroy me. Now, it is all over and it seems as if it were a bad dream.

All is past, Mother, and now all begins. When you called me on the telephone with words of consolation, for which I will always be grateful, you asked me this question: "What will you do with the life placed by force in your womb?"

I felt your voice tremble while asking this question to which there was no immediate answer. Not because I had not thought of the choice I had to make, but because you did not wish to cloud my decision. I have made my decision now. If I become a mother, the child will be mine and no one else's. I could entrust him to others, but he has the right to my motherly love, even though he was neither desired nor wanted.

We cannot separate a plant from its roots. The grain, fallen into the soil, needs to grow where the mysterious Sower scattered it. I ask nothing of my Congregation, which has already given me everything. I thank my sisters for their fraternal support, especially for not asking embarrassing questions. I will leave with my child. I do not know where, but God, who suddenly shattered my greatest joy, will show me which path to take to accomplish His will.

I will be poor. I will don once more the old apron and sabots which women wear on working days, and I will go with my mother to collect the resin from the pine trees in our forests. I will do everything in my power to break the chain of hatred that destroys our countries.

To the child I am expecting, I will teach only to love. My child, born from violence, will be a testimony that forgiveness is the unique greatness that glorifies a person.

. . . . . .

Here, in the destruction of a way of life and vocation, by the most hateful of crimes against a woman, is found the very essence, reason, and joy of the messages given by the Blessed Virgin at Medjugorje.

It is a seed that will yield more than a thousand-fold.

. . . . .

". . . My God, my God, why hast thou abandoned me?"
Matthew 27:46

Chapter 25

Oasis of Peace

What can be said of such a place as Medjugorje, which survives the all-destroying wrath of war? Only that it stands out starkly as miraculous in itself, a true oasis of peace.

After nearly three years of intense fighting, there had been no major damage or direct confrontational attacks in Medjugorje. Now, in January 1994, the war continued to rage throughout the region at a furious pace with action coming as close as three miles to the village. But the place of apparitions remained a cool spot of peace and safety in the midst of a storm.

Daily life continued. Mirjana and Ivanka both were expecting babies in the spring. It would be Ivanka's third and Mirjana's second. Marija was expecting her first child in July. For followers of the Medjugorje apparitions who were overly concerned with the predicted, impending chastisements, the growth of the families of these three visionaries served as a positive sign. Two of the visionaries had received all ten secrets from the Blessed Virgin. They knew what was coming, yet they chose to raise families. Mirjana would later be quoted as stating, "Those with large families will be better off."

As if to confirm this act of trust, the Blessed Virgin gave this monthly message in January 1994: *Dear children, you are all my little children. I love you. But, little children, you must not forget that without prayer you cannot be close to me. In this time, Satan wants to create disorder in your hearts and in your families. Little children, do not give in. You must not permit him to lead you and your life. I love you and intercede for you before God. Little children, pray!*

Once again, the Virgin was reconfirming her call for all who would listen to continue life as normal, but with prayer as the center. The lesson applied even more so in the time of war.

While spared physical damage, the village of Medjugorje suffered casualties. At least five soldiers from the community were killed on the front lines. Wives and mothers prayed for the safe return of fathers, sons, brothers, and husbands as they served periods of time on the front lines. All prayed for an end to this horrible disruption of daily life.

As if in response, Gospa gave this message in February: I thank you for your prayers. You all have helped me so that this war may finish as soon as possible. I am close to you and I pray for each one of you, and I beg you, Pray, Pray, Pray! Only through prayer we can defeat evil and protect all that which Satan wants to destroy in your life. I am your Mother and I love you all the same, and I intercede for you before God.

Even greater hardship became the norm of daily life. There were only a few hours of electricity and water each day, yet the faithful continued to turn out in large numbers for the evening Mass at Saint James Church. From Podbrdo Hill and the summit of Krizevac Mountain, organized groups prayed constantly for peace and for the soldiers. They had not lost their spirit.

The Madonna responded with this message in May: *I invite all of you to have more trust in me and to live my messages more deeply. I am with you and intercede before God for you, but also I wait for your hearts to open up to my messages. Rejoice because God loves you and gives you the possibility to convert everyday and to believe more in God, the Creator.*

The villagers were surprised to see such a large number of pilgrims from many different countries present in Medjugorje for the thirteenth anniversary of the apparitions. The Madonna gave this message through Marija as the faithful gathered in the village on June 25: *Dear children, today I rejoice in my heart at seeing you all present here. I bless you and I call you all to decide to live my messages which I give you here. I desire, little children, to guide you all to Jesus because He is your salvation. Therefore, little children, the more you pray, the more you will belong to me and to my Son Jesus. I bless you all with my motherly blessing and I thank you for having responded to my call.*

This anniversary was different in one respect: intermingled

with the visiting pilgrims were scores of refugees from war-torn areas. Most came because of relatives living in Medjugorje. New rooms built to house pilgrims now served as refugee living quarters. This was now their oasis of peace and safety, albeit a far cry from the security of homes and farms which had been held by families for decades. But it was better than the hastily erected refugee camps dotting the landscape, all of them critically short of essential food and medicine, and crowded beyond capacity with thousands of homeless victims.

While there were adequate food supplies available in Medjugorje, meat became scarce. Local sheep and cattle were butchered at alarming frequency to meet the needs of refugees. Out of this situation of shortage and necessity came a story about a most unique miracle, proving again that this little oasis of peace was special, holy ground.

The story goes that a villager named Josip had become modestly successful through the business of housing pilgrims during the early days of the apparitions. He had been one of the first to open his home to visiting pilgrims with no expectation of material gain. However, he was soon blessed with earnings far in excess of what he had earned by his own labors in the past.

Yet, Josip and his family continued living as they always had. His family was in attendance at the church each evening for the Mass, the apparition, and all of the prayers. He had been struck by the Blessed Virgin's message and was determined to live it to the best of his ability. Nothing had changed in the following years as his personal success increased. Josip knew and acknowledged where it had come from. He remained a man of prayer and fasting.

Success had allowed Josip to expand his home to take in more pilgrims, and to purchase material goods beyond his wildest expectations. Among his possessions was a large freezer that, during pre-war days, was always well stocked with freshly butchered meat. With the influx of refugee relatives, however, Josip's meat supply was fast dwindling, forcing him to butcher one of his cows.

He carefully wrapped the meat and placed it in the freezer, with the intention of rationing it sparingly. Soon, however, his neighbors had as great an overrun of refugee guests as he did. And they had no meat. So, Josip generously shared the meat with all in need, attempting to live the messages as he had since the Blessed Virgin had first appeared in the village.

Each day, Josip would take meat from the freezer for his family and his neighbors in need. The meat lasted far beyond the time when it would have run out. Yet, Josip was able to disperse the meat daily. Finally, a neighbor asked, "Josip, did you have to butcher your other cow?"

"No," Josip answered with a quiet smile, "it just keeps coming! Every time I open my freezer, there is the same amount of meat as the day I first butchered my cow."

Months later, Josip was *still* taking meat from his freezer. His explanation was simple and straightforward: "Gospa said we could stop wars with prayer and fasting, and that we could *alter the laws of nature . . .*"

. . . . .

The year ended with a noticeable decrease in the fighting. Food and medicine shortages continued; soldiers and civilians from all ethnic groups involved were still dying in war-related activities, including men from the village of Medjugorje. United Nations troops now stationed throughout the region were apparently ineffective in stopping small, ongoing skirmishes.

Small but deadly little battles raged not just against resisting pockets of insurgent Serbian forces, but now also between Croatians and Muslims. Initially, these two groups had been forced out of necessity to ally against the Serbs for survival and self-defense. Now, with thousands of ethnically cleansed Muslims descending and settling in Mostar and other areas that were predominantly Croatian enclaves, they were committing the same outrages against each other. Mostar, in particular, became a ferocious battleground.

Through it all, pilgrims continued to journey to the village, arriving with desperately needed clothing, food, and medicine. Medjugorje had become a major port of entry for these items, exceeding the amount of direct assistance of large charitable organizations. Many of the pilgrims—especially young people, predominantly from the United States, Italy and the United Kingdom—courageously traveled into active fighting areas to take vital supplies to refugees. They were not afraid; the Blessed Virgin Mary had assured them through her current messages that she would protect them in their mission to help the unfortunate victims. Not one pilgrim coming to Medjugorje during the active war years suffered injury or death as a direct result of combat.[12]

With a large group of pilgrims present in the village during the week of Christmas, the Blessed Virgin gave this Christmas Day message: *Dear children, today I am joyful with you and I pray with you for peace: Peace in your hearts, peace in your families, peace in your desires, and peace in the whole world. May the King of Peace bless you today and give you peace. I bless you and I carry each one of you in my heart.*

It was an answer only the faithful could fully comprehend.

. . . . .

You did not choose me, but I chose you and appointed you that you should go and bear fruit and that your fruit should abide; so that whatever you ask the Father in my name, he may give it to you. This I command you, to love one another.   John 15:16-17

---

12. Collette Webster, who was killed by a sniper in Mostar, did not come to Medjugorje as a pilgrim, but as a volunteer to assist the war victims.

PART V

The Harvest

*As he sat on the Mount of Olives, the disciples
came to him privately, saying, "Tell us . . . what
will be the sign of your coming and of the close
of the age?" And Jesus answered them, " . . . For
nation will rise against nation . . . and there will
be famines and earthquakes in various places:
all this is but the beginning of the sufferings.
Then they will deliver you up to tribulation . . .
And then many will fall away, and betray one
another, and hate one another. And many false
prophets will arise and lead many astray. And
because wickedness is multiplied, most men's
love will grow cold . . . For then there will be
great tribulation, such as has not been from the
beginning of the world until now, no, and never
will be. And if those days had not been shortened,
no human being would be saved; but for the sake
of the elect, those days will be shortened."*

Matthew 24: 3-12, 21-22

Chapter 26

Response

Thank you for having responded to my call.

These are the words the Blessed Virgin Mary uses to close each monthly message. No greater example of such response can be given than the incredible humanitarian actions taken by former and present Medjugorje pilgrims to assist the war victims.

Why would ordinary people interrupt the normal flow of daily life to go into an extremely dangerous war zone to take aid to people they do not know? Government agencies warned them of the dangers; friends and family members begged them not to do it. But the voice of the Blessed Virgin Mary rose above all the warnings as she called her children to help others in a time of urgent need.

The call was explicitly clear in her monthly messages given throughout the period of intense fighting. In February 1995, even as the war was mercifully winding down, she renewed her plea: *Today I invite you to become missionaries of my messages which I am giving here through this place that is dear to me. God has allowed me to stay this long with you and, therefore, little children, I invite you to live with love the messages I give, and to transmit them to the whole world so that a river of love flows to people who are full of hatred and without peace. I invite you, little children, to become peace where there is no peace and light where there is darkness, so that each heart accepts the light and the way of salvation.*

The brave, obedient souls entering into the inferno of conflict were attempting to live the messages. They were the signs of peace where there was no peace; they were the lights where there was no light. Without this direct aid by people spiritually charged through the apparitions of the Blessed Virgin Mary at Medjugorje, Bosnia would have become a desolate land of the living dead. Hundreds of thousands of innocent victims would have died from

147

neglect. Countless more would have been homeless.

The response was, and continues to be, an unconditional act of love. It is a direct answer to the Blessed Virgin's call to love as expressed in her April 1995 message: *I call you to love. Little children, without love you cannot live, neither with God nor with brother. Therefore, I call all of you to open your hearts to the love of God that is so great and open to each one of you. God, out of love for man, has sent me among you to show you the path of salvation, the path of love. If you do not first love God, then you will neither be able to love neighbor nor the one you hate. Therefore, little children, pray and through prayer you will discover love.*

It started with a "suitcase brigade." Pilgrims coming to Medjugorje were encouraged to bring something extra to assist the war victims. Medicine and clothing topped the list. Additional pieces of luggage began arriving with every pilgrimage, adding up to a sizeable amount of vital relief supplies.

Later, many pilgrimages included visits to nearby refugee centers where the pilgrims could personally deliver special gifts of love. Entire families were "adopted" by families whose pilgrim member might be among a tour. Regular, monthly financial support from these families brought stability to destitute refugees, allowing them time and resources to regain normalcy in daily life.

From this initial response, individuals stepped forth to form more organized efforts. Soon groups throughout the United States were working full-time to raise funds and supplies, filling large containers and sending them to Bosnia and Croatia by air and sea. Caritas of Birmingham, in Birmingham, Alabama, a lay-operated organization formed in 1986 specifically to spread the Medjugorje message, is an excellent example. They were soon delivering aid by containers two and three times a week. Caritas alone has been responsible for multiple millions of dollars in aid donated by people throughout the country. They continue their work up to the present time.

The efforts of Caritas of Birmingham spurred on others. In my own home town of Myrtle Beach, South Carolina, Bob Derr, deputy chief fireman, and Doctor Bill Greene, a urologist, combined talents and fervor with a few other people to obtain and refurbish six used ambulances and ship them to areas of Bosnia-Hercegovina and Croatia where they were vitally needed. Their project began with a few words during a visit to our area by Father Svetozar, who spoke about the war and the critical needs of the region. When asked what they could do to help, he mentioned the terrible shortage of ambulances.

Within a few months, Bob had scrounged around the country and come up with several dilapidated ambulances no longer in service. Both men traveled long distances to drive the ambulances to Myrtle Beach where they then secured the services of a local mechanic. They pitched in personally where they could to assist in preparing the vehicles for shipment overseas. Finally, not satisfied with this project alone, they sought out donated medical supplies (obtained through Doctor Greene's contacts with drug companies) and packed each ambulance to its limits prior to placing it in a shipping container.

The response to the Blessed Virgin's call was not just in the United States. In the United Kingdom, a converted Jew organized a relief network that sent millions of pounds of relief via truck convoys that included the trucks themselves so that the work could continue locally. Bernard Ellis developed his organization, the Medjugorje Appeal, to such a degree that convoys were leaving England for Bosnia two and three times a month. Two such convoys were manned by all women drivers. One of these was accompanied by Medjugorje visionary Ivan, while the other included the young American Collette Webster, who would later die a martyr's death at the hands of a sniper in Mostar.

Similar programs were underway in France, Italy, Germany, and Poland. The same was true in distant Australia, New Zealand, and other Far East nations. Even the little island nation of Bermuda, a few hundred miles off the coast of North Carolina, responded with many aid containers.

There are hundreds more such stories. Jeff Reed's story is typical. Jeff, a free-lance pilot living in Dallas, Texas, was first touched by Medjugorje while listening to a mother of twelve children give witness on how the apparitions had brought unity and conversion to her family. An Episcopalian by faith, with no special religious fervor, the flames of conversion were set ablaze in Jeff's heart by the woman's story. He began plowing through books and video-tapes and anything else having to do with Medjugorje. As a Protestant, Jeff had never known about the intercessory role of the Blessed Virgin Mary, or anything about apparitions; now, he couldn't get enough.

After attending a Medjugorje conference in Wichita, Kansas, and hearing a talk by Father Svetozar, who by this time was a well-traveled speaker on the Medjugorje conference schedule, Jeff was moved to go to Medjugorje. Knowing that Father Svet's main purpose at the conferences was to raise relief funds, Jeff traveled on to Konic, Father Svet's parish, to ask him what he could do personally to assist in the relief effort especially in the Konic region. He was disappointed when the good priest told him to pray, put it in God's hands and not make a campaign out of his efforts.

But the desire to help would not go away. He didn't have a clue where to start or how to raise money for a needy Catholic Church in Yugoslavia, especially since he was not Catholic. Jeff sought the advice of four people who were good friends and associates. One of them advised him to contact me, knowing I was close to Father Svet and the situation in that region.

I was speaking in the Basilica of the Immaculate Conception, in Washington, D.C., when first approached by Jeff. He had journeyed to the conference in hopes of meeting with me, with no prior contact. Somehow, we came together for a brief five minutes. The young pilot poured out his story and asked me what he should do to get started. To his dismay, I told him almost the same thing Father Svet had said. He needed to pray and if it was meant to be . . .

Jeff was crushed—and now very confused. The desire to help the church and war victims in Konic was still burning bright, but my words did not contain the answers he was seeking. Utterly discouraged, Jeff nevertheless went below the Basilica into one of the many chapels to pray, just as he had been told to do. He had never prayed so intensely in his life, asking the Blessed Virgin over and over to allow him to actively assist in the relief effort. If that meant sweeping floors or digging ditches, that was okay, as long as she would allow him to work for her Son. Suddenly, he received a clear message from the Blessed Mother: *I already have.*

Seven days later, Jeff was startled to receive a check in the mail from one of the four people with whom he had sought advice. The check was for $50,000. There was a note included: "If Medjugorje can change you, it can change anybody." It went on to state that the money was to help him get started in his relief work.

As far as Jeff was concerned, this was the start *and* the finish; he left shortly thereafter and delivered most of the money to Father Svet in Konic, doing so under a special fund account set up through his Episcopal church. Little did he know what else God had in mind for St. David's Fund.

With the escalation of the war throughout Croatia, and later Bosnia, Jeff took the remainder of the money in the St. David's Fund and began organizing relief work. The fund later became an independent, non-profit organization called St. David's Relief Foundation. To date, in excess of 8.5 million dollars in aid has been raised and sent to Bosnia and Croatia. Operating with a small staff, the Foundation continues to deliver a container load of relief supplies approximately every two weeks.

As for Jeff, as long as people continue to respond, he will continue his efforts. When they stop, he will know that God has something else for him to do.

. . . . .

And he said, "The kingdom of God is as if a man should scatter seed upon the ground, and should sleep and rise night and day, and the seed should sprout and grow, he knows not how. The earth produces of itself, first the blade, then the ear, then the full grain in the ear. But when the grain is ripe, at once he puts in the sickle, because the harvest has come."　　　　　Mark 4:26-29

Chapter 27

From Darkness to Light

The response continued. Charity was evident everywhere as physicians, dentists, nurses, and a wide variety of professionals came to the area to donate time and equipment, and help the homeless and sick. A calm but steady intensity filled all efforts to reestablish the village and the surrounding area in that special, unique peace that had marked it so strongly before the war.

On March 18, 1995, the Blessed Virgin expressed deep concern in an admonishing message to Mirjana during her annual apparition. It was a strong call to action: *Dear children, as a mother for many years now, I am teaching you faith and love for God. Neither have you shown gratitude to the dear Father, nor have you given Him glory. You have become empty and your heart has become hard, and without love for the sufferings of your neighbors. I am teaching you love, and I am showing you that the dear Father has loved you, but you have not loved Him. He sacrificed His Son for your salvation, my children. For as long as you do not love, you will not come to know the love of your Father. You will not come to know Him because God is Love. Love, and have no fear, my children, because in love there is no fear. If your hearts are open to the Father and if they are full of love towards Him, why then fear what is to come? Those who do not love are afraid because they expect punishment and because they know how empty and hard they are. I am leading you, children, towards love, towards the dear Father. I am leading you into Eternal Life. Eternal Life is my Son. Accept Him and you will have accepted Love.* [emphasis added]

The apparition lasted ten minutes. The Virgin's face was serious but radiating with love and intensity; tears of emotion flowed from Mirjana. The message was clear and direct: More had to be done to alleviate the suffering of the innocent victims of war.

A year later, the same intensity was again strongly reflected in the Blessed Virgin Mary's annual message to Mirjana: *Dear chil-*

dren! On this message, which I give you today through my servant, I desire for you to reflect a long time. My children, great is the love of God! Do not close your eyes, do not close your ears while I repeat to you: Great is His love! Hear my call and my supplication, which I direct to you. Consecrate your heart and make in it the home of the Lord. May He dwell in it forever. My eyes and my heart will be here, even when I will no longer appear. Act in everything as I ask you and lead you to the Lord. Do not reject from yourself the name of God, that you may not be rejected. Accept my messages that you may be accepted. Decide, my children; it is the time of decision. Be just and innocent of heart, that I may lead you to your Father, for this, that I am here, is His great love.

. . . . .

All around the village of Medjugorje are the signs that people have responded to the Blessed Virgin's call. On the other side of the valley, there is a small collection of newly constructed, multi-unit houses, and a beautiful new school building. It is an orphanage founded by Father Slavko Barbaric and run by Franciscan sisters. The rooms in the home are warm and modern, creating as close to a normal home atmosphere as possible. The orphans are those of parents killed in the war.

The orphanage opened without a lot of fanfare. There was no international effort to raise funds for its construction. There was no special assistance from the government or international charities. It was simply another project, badly needed, taken on by the Franciscans, the villagers, and the visiting pilgrims. It continues today, supported by many pilgrims and locals. It gives light to the lives and futures of these children. Before, there was only darkness.

Just beyond Podbrdo Hill sitting near the home of visionary Marija and her husband Paolo, is a complex of buildings surrounded by a high stone wall. Originally a drug rehabilitation center, today it serves as far more than that. It is for the "poor in spirit": the alcoholic, the displaced, the destitute whose lives have been shattered by the ongoing war of evil against good. Today, the former drug rehabilitation center is known as the "School of Life."

Sister Elvira, an Italian nun who is responsible for twenty-seven similar centers in eight countries, opened the center in June

1991. The diminutive but dynamic religious, from her very first days in Medjugorje, was certain that such a center was the right response to the Blessed Virgin's appeal. It now stands as every day proof that the phenomenon of Medjugorje is an authentic request from heaven for the conversion of sinners. Hundreds of drug addicts have occupied the premises since its opening.

At first, there was nothing more than Sister Elvira's dream; then, the acquisition of a piece of rock-strewn property. A large tent provided accommodations for the fledgling center. There was no water or electricity. The charter residents began digging and building, using the stones in the ground for the building blocks of the walls and floors. Today, the present occupants continue the work.

It is extremely hard work. Each day begins with prayer and Holy Mass, followed by a light breakfast; then, a full day of physical labor follows, no matter the weather conditions. This is the only treatment plan. There are no doctors, psychologists, or nursing aides. There are no medications or withdrawal drugs for the addicts or alcoholics. There is no entertainment—no television or radios; no cigarettes or alcohol. There is nothing but prayer, love, and hard work.

The cure rate for the drug addicts is an astounding ninety-percent. The spiritual conversion rate is even higher. Those accepted into the program are required to stay a minimum of three years, with a request that they remain an additional two years to serve others coming into the program. Yet, they are free to leave at any time. If they stay, they must follow the regimen to the letter. There is no fee; everything is supported by charitable donations.

Today, the center is a sprawling complex. The residents make a variety of gifts that may be purchased by visitors, who now include nearly all pilgrimages coming to Medjugorje. And, Sister Elvira has added to her work by opening a small house for women suffering the same malaise of a world guided only by materialism and civil laws.

. . . . .

Recently, I became actively involved with a special charity in Medjugorje whose purpose is to assist homeless war refugees by providing them with houses. It is yet another example of the call to put into action what the Blessed Virgin Mary is asking in her messages.

The formation of this charity began in a simple way. Zvonko Coja and his family desperately needed a place to live. They had been ethnically cleansed from their home by Muslim Slavs during the war. They had lived in a town named Konice, bordering the city of Sarajevo. His brother's wife was shot and killed, and a brother-in-law captured and savagely tortured by Muslim troops who cut off his ears and nose and gouged out his eyes. Zvonko fled to Medjugorje with his wife and three small children. With the assistance of Father Svet, whom he had known through the Catholic Church in Konice where Father Svet had served, he was given a temporary place to stay.

Zvonko's family settled in a tiny shack next door to Ante Music who, after a strong spiritual conversion, had moved to Medjugorje fifteen years earlier from his home town of Split in Croatia. Seeing the desperation of his new neighbor, Ante wanted to do something to help him. He began to formulate plans to raise funds to build a permanent home for Zvonko's family.

Ante had served as an English-speaking guide in Medjugorje for many years. It was through this service that he met and later married his Irish wife, Paula, who was the daughter of a well-known Irish author and journalist, Heather Parsons. Heather had written a book about Medjugorje and led Irish pilgrimages there. When Heather came for a visit and learned of the new neighbor's plight, she wanted to help. Between them all, they began planning for a special event back in Ireland that might raise enough funds to build a home for Zvonko and his family.

In 1998, Patricia Keane made the pilgrimage to Medjugorje, where she also felt a powerful spiritual conversion. Upon returning home, she met Heather, who lived in the same town, learned of her desire to assist the refugee family living next to her daughter, and decided to become involved. In short time, Patricia took the lead and expanded the effort to try and help other desperate refugee families. From this beginning, Rebuild For Bosnia was officially established in early 1999.

Final Harvest

It was later that same year that I met Patricia Keane at Medjugorje. She explained the purpose of the charity and that they were now working to build as many homes as possible to provide for other refugees. Would I help, she asked? Would I agree to be the patron of the charity? Normally, I would have declined giving as a reason that I had my own mission to take care of. Once again, however, there was that inner urge that I was to become involved in this work. I agreed, and immediately started formulating ways to raise funds for the project.

Patricia, working closely with Ante in Medjugorje as the front man, soon had hired a construction company that could erect prefabricated homes in approximately forty days, at a cost of about 15,000 Irish pounds. Zvonko and his family were the first to receive a new home; by the late summer of 2001, there were approximately thirty homes finished and occupied, or under construction. The charity, now a full time job for Patricia, is surging in growth and the goal now is to build an entire village for refugees. Ironically, the construction company being employed to build the prefabricated homes is a Muslim construction company—the same ethnic group that ran Zvonko and other Catholic families out of Konice. There is healing taking place among the builders and the grateful refugees; and, there is no partiality concerning ethnic background. The charity builds homes for Croatian Catholics, Serbian Orthodox, and Muslim refugee families. The only qualification is being a victim of the horror of war.

After writing about Rebuild For Bosnia in our monthly newsletter and speaking about it in my talks, we began to accumulate funds. I decided to take it a step further. I was leading a pilgrimage to Medjugorje in November 2000 and had sent a letter to each pilgrim asking for donations of essential toiletries and clothing. The group brought large suitcases full of these items and we distributed them to the waiting families who were still living in squalid conditions. More importantly, the pilgrims generously donated toward the building of a house. That was my goal: to collect enough funds from this group of pilgrims to build at least one home as a permanent legacy for this particular pilgrimage.

After speaking about the charity in my opening talk, I was approached by a couple from the group the following day. "We'd

156

like to donate a house," the husband told me, "but we ask that you keep our names confidential."

I was not sure if I had heard him right. "You mean you want to make a contribution?" I asked.

"No," he said, "we want to donate an entire house!"

I was nearly speechless—and immediately filled with emotion. I couldn't thank them enough and, later, in the evening talks, I told the others in our group about the extraordinary offer. Soon two more people came forward and pledged to work toward obtaining funds so that they, too, could donate a full house. How amazing it is that the more one prays and trusts in God, the more He gives.

Several days later, the first couple who had promised to donate a house approached me again and said they would match each house pledged by the rest of the group! The result was that this pilgrimage left a legacy of at least four homes, with a strong possibility of two more from donations that continue to come in from members of the pilgrimage.

I returned home from this, my 33rd pilgrimage to Medjugorje, spiritually refreshed and filled with renewed fervor to live the messages of Our Lady.

. . . . .

Then the King will say to those at his right hand, 'Come, O blessed of my Father, inherit the kingdom prepared for you from the foundation of the world; for I was hungry and you gave me food, I was thirsty and you gave me drink, I was a stranger and you welcomed me, I was naked and you clothed me, I was sick and you visited me, I was in prison and you came to me.'

Matthew 25:34-36

Chapter 28

Fulfillment

In September 1998, another major event brought the apparitions a step closer to fulfillment. While Jakov and Mirjana were fulfilling a round of speaking engagements in the United States, Jakov received his final, daily apparition with the Blessed Virgin; he also received the tenth secret.

The Blessed Virgin came to Jakov on September 12, in Miami, Florida, where he was vacationing with his family and giving talks on Medjugorje. With a gentle smile, she said to him: *Dear child, I am your mother and I love you unconditionally. From today, I will not be appearing to you every day, but only on Christmas, the birthday of my Son. Do not be sad, because as a mother, I will always be with you and like every true mother, I will never leave you. And you continue further to follow the way of my Son, the way of peace and love, and try to persevere in the mission that I have confided to you. Be an example of that man who has known God and God's love. Let people always see in you an example of how God acts on people and how God acts through them. I bless you with my motherly blessing and I thank you for having responded to my call.*

Jakov cried for a long time. He had cried most of the previous day when the Blessed Virgin had first told him that the next day would be his final, daily apparition. The jocular Jakov was subdued as he traveled in the Southern Florida region giving talks. Several days later, he traveled to the poverty-stricken nation of Haiti, where more than 70,000 people came to hear the message of Medjugorje. A quieter, mature Jakov was beginning a new phase of service as a witness of how God acts on people—and through them.

With Jakov's final apparition, that left three of the original six visionaries still receiving daily apparitions, while the Virgin continued to appear at least once annually to the other three. All but

Vicka now were married, with Ivan marrying an American, Laureen Murphy, in October 1994. They now have three children. The family theme remains strong into the new century, as the grace of the Virgin's daily apparitions continues.

. . . . . .

On a mild, early November afternoon in 1998, more than 700 pilgrims gathered in the huge, newly constructed hall some 200 yards behind Saint James Church. They were there for a talk I was giving primarily for English-speaking pilgrims. But word had spread, and many foreign groups were also present. The presence of so many pilgrims was visible proof that after more than seventeen years of daily apparitions by the Blessed Virgin Mary, good fruits continued to flow from Medjugorje.

I had brought a pilgrimage of 220 people from across the United States. As I began speaking, a feeling of humility and awe filled my heart. Each talk always seemed as if it were the first; in nearly fourteen years of traveling the world speaking about the message of Medjugorje, it had never become routine or dull for me.

There was a family in our group with an astounding eighteen members present. I asked them to stand. The widowed mother had brought her children and their spouses and children to Medjugorje as a family unit, spending what she called her "inheritance" to do so. She was convinced there was nothing better she could give them for their future. They clearly served as a powerful symbol of the family values theme that runs through the Blessed Virgin's messages.

A young Lutheran pastor and his wife were also in our group. I also asked them to stand. They represented the ecumenical outreach of the Blessed Mother, who constantly emphasizes her untiring desire to bring all of her children to her Son.

I then asked how many pilgrims were in Medjugorje for the first time. Incredibly, all but a few hands were thrust in the air. A low murmur ran through the crowd. "Do you realize," I asked them, pausing for a moment, "that the Blessed Virgin Mary has waited seventeen years, four months, and a few days for you to come to Medjugorje? Are you aware that the miracles, signs, and wonderment of the beginning days of the apparitions are just as abundant for you today as they have been for pilgrims since the beginning of the apparitions?"

The low murmur exploded into applause. The point was clear to this large gathering of pilgrims: Medjugorje at this juncture was the same as Medjugorje in the early eighties.

. . . . .

With a merciful end of active war, a tentative peace prevailed. But signs of the "Storm" were still very evident. Our group traveled by bus to Mostar to celebrate Mass in the new chapel at the Franciscan monastery. The trip allowed us an up-close look at the fruits of war. We passed the cathedral with its roof still caved in from the shelling that pounded the city during the height of war in 1992. The bishop's home, which had suffered similar damage, had at least been restored and was once again occupied.

Our buses rolled past cemeteries expanded beyond original boundaries with hundreds of new tombstones. Many beautiful parks had been turned into cemeteries to accommodate the overload of casualties. Thousands of bullet marks riddled the walls of standing buildings, while others lay in ruins, serving as constant reminders that aid was still desperately needed. It would be needed for years to come.

A drizzle of rain fell, making the mood of our trip even more somber. The buses parked in a makeshift lot near the new church building still under construction and a good distance from the chapel. We trekked in silence to the monastery. I was reminded of an earlier visit here with Father Svet during the war, when we literally had to run this gauntlet from doorway to doorway to avoid the danger of snipers hidden in the surrounding bombed-out buildings.

By the time I reached the chapel, it was filled. Feeling a bit annoyed, I wondered aloud why we were assembling in this smaller chapel when there was a much larger sanctuary in the basement of the main church presently being used by the parishioners. One of our guides, Slavenka, a striking Croatian woman with blazing red hair, assured me with a smile, "Don't worry, it will hold us all. It is no different than being in Saint James Church for the evening Mass."

She was right. While there was hardly room to move, we all managed to find a niche. Eventually, annoyance was replaced with peace. It was as if we could sense the full force of peace in this special place that had arisen out of the darkness of the war. Because of the location of the chapel, it was one of the holiest and most peaceful times of our pilgrimage. Here we were surrounded by the remnants of the unpeace that had prevailed for so long.

After the Mass, I spoke briefly, reminding the pilgrims that they were seeing firsthand the total absence of love. This was visible evidence of the diseased fruit of Satan, who is always present where Mary is sent, to try and snatch away the grace. I reminded them that the battle was not just that played out in the killing fields of active combat. The battle was within each of us. It is the constant battle of good against evil. That is why Medjugorje continues today, I told them. This pilgrimage was a reminder, as were all of the others, that the battle rages on until every possible soul has the opportunity to say "yes" or "no" to God's gifts of grace.

. . . . . .

The village of Medjugorje looked different than it did on my first pilgrimage in May 1986. Aesthetic and practical improvements had been made to the church grounds, including the new hall and other new buildings for meetings and special services. But for the most part, the villagers were the same, and the pilgrims coming from countries throughout the world were the same. Attendance was still overflowing at the evening program of the rosary followed by Holy Mass.

Commercialism was everywhere, of course, but that was to be expected. Humanity's original stain will always be part of any supernatural spiritual event. Without it, one should be suspect. There are no "short-cuts" in the spiritual life; the choice of good over evil is there for each to make.

The Blessed Virgin had reminded the people during Mirjana's annual apparition in March 1997, that we have a choice as to which path we take: *Dear children! As a mother, I ask that you do not go on the path that you have been on; that is the path without love towards neighbor and towards my Son. On this path, you will find only hardness and emptiness of heart, and not peace, which you all long for. Truthful peace will have only that one, who in his neighbor sees and loves my son. In the heart of the one where only my Son reigns, that one knows what peace and security is.*

She followed this with a powerful reminder in her monthly message on the sixteenth anniversary of the apparitions, June 25, 1997: *Today, I am with you in a special way, and I bring you my motherly blessing of peace. I pray for you and I intercede for you before God, so that you may comprehend that each of you is a carrier of peace. You cannot have peace if your heart is not at peace with God. That is why, little children, pray, pray, pray, because prayer is the foundation of your peace. Open your heart and give time to God so that He will be your friend. When true friendship with God is realized, no storm can destroy it.*

The "Storm" would always be part of Medjugorje's story. While active war had ceased and the battle for souls continued, opposition to the apparitions raged on. It had begun with the bishop of Mostar, Pavao Zanic (retired since 1991), who rejected the apparitions after at first embracing them with zeal. His successor, Ratko Peric, is even more opposed. The reason is the same: the age-old conflict between Franciscans and secular priests for control of parishes within the diocese. After seventeen-plus years of incredible spiritual fruits, this remained the singular basis for opposition to the apparitions.

An amusing aside was told me by one of the Franciscans. Retired Bishop Zanic was recently asked by a priest favorable to the apparitions, "Bishop, after all of these years and the thousands of conversions, what do you think about Medjugorje now?"

Bishop Zanic paused and then said, "I've been thinking a lot about that these days . . ."

Even with this little beam of enlightenment in the mind of a formidable opponent, questions must be asked: Are the opponents of the apparitions blind? Can they not hear or understand? Are six unsophisticated teenagers—now young adults, most of them married and parents—capable of maintaining a pretense of seeing a heavenly visitor for more than twenty years? Could such a fabricated story, masterminded by the Franciscans, as the two bishops seem to believe, give rise to millions of conversions to Jesus Christ across the entire world?

No apparition has ever had as large an impact on the world as Medjugorje. How could an act of the devil—as other opponents label Medjugorje—lead to renewal of whole dioceses, creation of thousands of prayer groups, reconciliation of thousands of families and the motivation for so many priestly and religious vocations?

The answer lies in the book of truth, Holy Scripture: ". . . because seeing they do not see, and hearing they do not hear, nor do they understand. With them indeed is fulfilled the prophecy of Isaiah which says: 'You shall indeed hear but never understand, and you shall indeed see but never perceive. For this people's heart has grown dull . . .'"

And for those who do believe because of the good fruits: "But blessed are your eyes, for they see, and your ears, for they hear. Truly, I say to you, many prophets and righteous men longed to see what you see, and did not see it, and to hear what you hear, and did not hear it."[13]

Where does Medjugorje presently stand with the Church? In August 1996, Dr. Joaquin Navarro-Valls, spokesman for the Holy See, issued a public statement in answer to charges that the faithful were being disobedient in going to Medjugorje: "You cannot say people cannot go until it has been proven false. This has not been said, so anyone can go if they want."

That statement holds true today as pilgrims continue to visit Medjugorje on pilgrimage. Throughout the year 2001, pilgrimages grew in size and number; the anniversary on June 25, 2001, was by many estimates the largest anniversary crowd in the history of the apparitions. The same could be said concerning the youth festival held the following month in which more than 10,000 youths, and in excess of 20,000 pilgrims, filled every part of Medjugorje.

---

13. Matthew 13:13-17.

The apparitions remain under investigation by the bishops of Bosnia-Hercegovina, although activity in this regard is basically dormant. A ruling on authenticity will not be issued until the apparitions have ended and the investigation is completed. However, due to its good fruits, Medjugorje is officially accepted as a shrine, a special place of prayer and worship.

Even Pope John Paul II has unofficially spoken in glowing terms of Medjugorje. Retired U.S. Bishop Sylvester Treinen told a Medjugorje conference crowd in excess of 7,000 that when he told the Holy Father he had just come from Medjugorje, His Holiness responded, "Yes, it is good for pilgrims to go to Medjugorje and do penance. It is good!"

The "Storm" subsides only when we listen with open hearts to the Blessed Virgin's words: *Dear children, do not forget: this is a time of grace; that is why, pray, pray, pray! Thank you for having responded to my call.* (October 1999)

Thus, right up to the present time, she reaffirms the heart of her mission: Prayer. The good fruits of the harvest continue.

. . . . .

So in the present case I tell you, keep away from these men and let them alone; for if this plan or this undertaking is of men, it will fail; but if it is of God, you will not be able to overthrow them. You might even be found opposing God!   Acts 5:38-39

Chapter 29

Final Harvest

Comparatively little has been said up to this point about the ten secrets given to the visionaries. The reason is simple. The Blessed Mother tells us to focus on the love, peace, and grace of the apparitions and not be too concerned with the secrets beyond knowing about them. In an early message in answer to questions about the secrets, she replied: *Place them in your mind and in your heart, and then pray for the conversion of the world.*

At Fatima, once it was learned that the "third" secret would not be released, everyone wanted to know what it was. In fact, as we have stated, the third secret was a part of the overall secret. Nevertheless, after the third part of the secret was released, after decades of people petitioning and feverishly campaigning for it to be revealed, interest dwindled immediately. There was disappointment that "more" was not contained in the secret. Yet, as we have seen, the full Fatima secret is a powerful call to repentance and prayer for the salvation of souls. What "more" could be wanted?

The Blessed Virgin's point is, if we live the messages, we have no reason to be curious or fear for the future. In the time of final harvest, focus should be on personal conversion to the ways of God. The purpose of her long visit to us at Medjugorje is to allow all people the opportunity to find this true peace and happiness. What if we knew the contents of all of the secrets? What would we do? Would we not pray and fast in hopes that all of our family and friends would respond by converting to God? Yet, this is just what we are called to now—without having to know what the secrets contain. Knowing or not knowing is not the point; living the messages is what is needed.

We are given signs and wonders in Medjugorje so that we may understand and accept that this entire event comes from God. The Blessed Virgin gave us so many signs in the early days, signs that continue to this day. The miracle of the sun still occurs in Medjugorje, and, incredibly, many people who have been touched by Medjugorje are able to see this miracle on occasion in their own communities when they return home.

Most pilgrims move beyond the signs. They thank God for what they have experienced, and then we try to put the messages to work in daily life. They see, they acknowledge, and then they move forward spiritually. These are the souls who will be among the final harvest.

There are other wondrous signs given throughout the world. Several years ago, I learned about one while in El Paso, Texas, for a speaking engagement. On the second day, with a little time off in the morning, several people from the group that sponsored my tour planned a trip for us into Juarez, Mexico, right across the border.

As we crossed the border, there were few changes in the landscape. Then, little by little, we could see the abject poverty of this region of Mexico: the poor, shabby buildings and homes, the roads in desperate need of repair. We went into such a neighborhood to visit the home of a couple living in this poverty, but who had been blessed with a miracle of hope.

The couple had been a typical example of the breakdown of family life: they were living together, unmarried, in poverty and depression. The man was an alcoholic who often went into fits of exasperated rage brought on by the cross of being poor. In his fury, he frequently beat the woman. She had been brought up as a believer, but gradually her faith had grown lukewarm, and she fell headlong into this pitiful situation.

In desperation to escape the horror of her daily life, the woman purchased a large picture of the Sacred Heart of Jesus at a local flea market. It was tattered and stained. She bought it, spurred on by faint memories of her childhood faith. Maybe, she thought, if she took it home and prayed to Jesus, her man would change.

The woman placed the picture on a small table in her bedroom and began to pray. Suddenly, she noticed blood running down the picture, issuing slowly from the Sacred Heart of Jesus vividly depicted in the picture. It was actual blood, and it was flowing profusely. Shocked, the woman called the man into the bedroom to see this miracle. In seconds, both fell to their knees, rubbing their eyes, overwhelmed with what they were seeing. Amid weeping and wonderment, they began to pray in earnest.

A short time later, with the miraculous bleeding still occurring, the man stopped drinking and stopped beating the woman. The couple began attending mass, went to confession, and shortly thereafter, they were married in the Church.

Word of the miracle spread amongst the poor of the region. People came from everywhere to the run-down, little neighborhood to see the wondrous sign of the bleeding heart of Jesus Christ. Priests came, the local bishop came, and scientists came. No one could explain why the picture bled. The blood was analyzed and discovered to be human blood. The heart in the picture would bleed most profusely on Thursdays and on holy feast days. Thousands came and continue to come to this day as the bleeding continues.

My friends and I also came to see this marvelous sign. After introductions to the woman who had purchased the picture and erected the little shrine, we knelt in front of it and began to pray the rosary. I sensed in my heart that this was a true sign. As we prayed, I felt the Blessed Virgin asking me to leave a medal she had blessed during an apparition in Medjugorje.

Concluding our prayers, I gave the woman a medal, telling her I wanted to leave another near the picture. Through the translator, she replied that she was happy with this and asked if I might lay the medal instead at a small altar in the house. We went inside where the woman had a small altar with a little piece of red velvet covering it and a crucifix lying on top. I laid the medal near the crucifix and said a quick prayer.

As we prepared to leave, one of the women from our group, not satisfied with where I had placed the medal, picked it up to move it closer to the crucifix. Suddenly, she let out a scream and told us to come quickly and look. The medal from Medjugorje that I had just moments ago placed near the crucifix was now bleeding!

Why would God give such signs as these? A bleeding picture, and a bleeding medal? Possibly, it may be because, even after twenty years of miracles surrounding Medjugorje, there are still so many people who do not know that God exists, who still have not been touched by His love. There are millions of people throughout the world who do not know the peace, grace and love that flow from the miracle of Medjugorje.

The messages from the Virgin of Medjugorje are not about punishment; they are about love and mercy. She does not come in apparition for one individual or one denomination. She comes for all of the separated brethren who call themselves Christian, Jew or Muslim. She comes for all of the followers of God. She comes to bring us together as one family under one God.

The secrets are not just about chastisements. We already have chastisements. We have abortion, drugs, divorce, alcoholism, suicide . . . Truly, we are living the sorrowful mysteries of the rosary. We are in agony, and we are suffering the scourging at the pillar. We are wearing the crown of thorns; we are staggering under the weight of the cross. We are approaching the crucifixion. We see it in our churches, our daily life, our families, and our nation. We are not blind.

And we remain divided in so many ways, especially spiritually, broken into countless religions and philosophies of life. We are divided because we have abandoned God and His laws, replacing them with self-serving civil laws. We heap indignities upon ourselves as we scratch, claw and connive to achieve the best and the most for ourselves. We want the richest material goods and absolute power to go along with them.

In truth, we Americans can no longer say, "In God we trust." We should say, rather, "In civil law we trust." Civil law, raised to secular holiness, has given us the "freedom" to deny God and His laws. It has legitimized the heinous killing of innocent children in the womb; it has created endless loopholes for businesses to cheat, and for individuals to bear false witness. It has allowed us to covet what others have in the name of success. In short, civil law has made it possible for us to break *every* commandment of God!

A little less than seventy years ago, mainstream Protestant churches accepted contraception as a legitimate practice. It was understood as an application of human intelligence—a gift of God—to reasonably limit a family's number of children. In 1973, that "acceptance" was disastrously increased beyond measure when the right to procured abortion was sanctioned by the Supreme Court. Thus, contraception entered into a new, far more lethal stage. Thirty years later, under the protection of civil law, *more than 50 million* abortions have been performed in the United States alone. And if we take that figure—a conservative figure— and add it to the number of abortions performed worldwide in this period, the total is beyond staggering! Only now is the awesome reality beginning to register.

We still do not seem to understand how division within God's family happened. We do not understand the schism that first split the Church, nearly a thousand years ago, into East and West, into Roman Catholic and Orthodox. We do not understand the heretical exodus of millions of the faithful over 482 years ago that established Protestantism during the so-called reformation of a corrupt church hierarchy.

It was not irreparable differences in theology or far-flung geographical separation that caused these divisions. Nor was it one man or one cause. The division then and now is the work of Satan, plain and simple. He uses the weaknesses of men to divide and conquer. He uses pride, greed, and lust to stir up division in individual hearts and in society. By means of this persistent "divide and conquer" strategy, he defaces the image and likeness of God in man and prevents him from knowing the Father's love.

In her messages at Medjugorje, the Blessed Virgin has given us the formula for being among the final harvest of souls. That is why God has granted the overwhelming grace of allowing the human mother of Jesus to come to us for so long a time. She is telling us that this is the time when we must truly choose between God and Satan, this is the hour when we must put our hands on the Cross with Jesus. She will not come to us indefinitely. The time is now.

Soon, there will be just one visionary at Medjugorje still receiving daily apparitions from the Blessed Virgin. Then, there will be none. When the last apparition takes place, there will be a brief period of time before the secrets begin to unfold. For those who believe, it will be a time of joy—not apprehension or fear. It will be a fulfillment of what the Blessed Virgin Mary said in the early days of Medjugorje: *When I have appeared for the final time to the last visionary of Medjugorje, I will no longer come in apparition to earth again, because it will no longer be necessary.*

For those who choose not to believe the grace of the apparitions, it will be too late.

When will the Blessed Virgin make her final appearance at Medjugorje? After more than two decades of daily apparitions, is the time near? The answers lie only with God, but this much is known: The Blessed Virgin promised Lucia, the last remaining visionary of Fatima, that she would live to see the fulfillment of the secrets of Fatima. Lucia is in her late eighties. She has reportedly stated that Medjugorje's apparitions are a *fulfillment* of the secrets of Fatima.

I conclude this chapter with a message given in September 1988, in Lourdes, to Father Stefano Gobbi. It underscores perfectly the Virgin's urgent, on-going call for conversion at Medjugorje: . . . *On this day, I ask you to consecrate to me the whole of the time which still separates you from the end of this century of yours. It is a period of ten years. They are ten very important years. They are ten decisive years. I ask you to spend them with me, because you are entering into the final period of the Second Advent, which is leading you to the triumph of my Immaculate Heart in the glorious coming of my Son Jesus.*

The Blessed Virgin Mary is speaking of a period of time that began more than thirteen years ago! Thus, we are already in the final period of the Second Advent. She continued: *In this period of ten years the fullness of time which I have pointed out to you, beginning with La Salette right up to my most recent and current apparitions, will be completed . . . In this period of ten years, the purification, which you have been living through for years, will come to its peak, and therefore sufferings will become all the greater for everyone . . . In this period of ten years, the time of the great tribulation, which was foretold to you by divine Scripture, before the second coming of Jesus, will be completed . . . In this period of ten years, the mystery of iniquity will be manifested, prepared for by the ever-increasing spread of apostasy . . .*

And then this: *In this period of ten years, all the secrets which I have revealed to some of My children will be fulfilled and all the events which have been foretold to you by Me will come to pass . . .*

More than 13 years have passed since this message was given, and yet, Medjugorje continues with its daily apparitions. What does this mean? Are the Marian Movement of Priests messages false, misleading, wrong? If this pointed message is true, why have the secrets of Medjugorje not occurred? Such are the questions posed by critics of Medjugorje and of the Marian Movement of Priests.

A closer look, however, sheds light on the relevance and splendor of these texts. The Virgin refers to secrets which she revealed to some of her children, not necessarily to *all* of her children.[14] And, as noted in an earlier chapter, all such prophecies are conditional, that is, dependent on the response of the children of God. They can be delayed, hastened, or mitigated just as the seventh secret of Medjugorje was mitigated.

The permanent sign at Medjugorje—and I personally think, at other Marian apparition sites—will come soon; and, the world will know the full truth of God's miracles not only at Medjugorje but throughout the ages. Many will say for the first time: "My God, you are real!"

After the signs and fulfillment of the secrets of Medjugorje, the world will be fresh, clean and pure again. And we shall then live as men lived in ancient times.

. . . . .

Then I looked, and lo, a white cloud, and seated on the cloud one like a son of man, with a golden crown on his head, and a sharp sickle in his hand. And another angel came out of the temple, calling with a loud voice to him who sat upon the cloud, "Put in your sickle, and reap, for the hour to reap has come, for the harvest of the earth is fully ripe." So he who sat upon the cloud swung his sickle on the earth, and the earth was reaped.

Revelation 14:14-16

---

14. The Blessed Virgin is speaking about those children chosen to be visionaries at the various apparition sites during the past two centuries, specifically, I believe, at La Salette and Fatima.

Chapter 30

Into the 21st Century

As the new century dawned, visionaries Marija, Ivan and Vicka were still receiving daily apparitions from the Blessed Virgin— they continue to do so to the present hour. Similarly, Ivanka enjoys a visit from the Blessed Virgin on June 25 of each year, and Jakov on Christmas day. Mirjana continues to receive apparitions on the second day of each month in addition to an annual visit and message on her birthday, March 18.

All of the visionaries and locutionists, except Jelena, are now married with budding families. In the fall of 2001, followers of Medjugorje were astounded by the announcement that Vicka, also, would marry the following January. At present, Ivan travels throughout the world to speak about the apparitions and his involvement. Marija, Ivanka and Mirjana also travel to witness, but only when family time allows it.

As the daily apparitions continued into the second year of the new century, the Virgin reaffirmed the foundation of her call with this lucid message given to visionary Marija on February 25, 2001: *Dear children! Wake up from the sleep of unbelief and sin, because this is a time of grace which God gives you. Use this time and seek the grace of healing of your heart from God, so that you may see God and man with the heart. Pray in a special way for those who have not come to know God's love, and witness with your life so that they also can come to know God and His immeasurable love. Thank you for having responded to my call.*

Through such direct, supernatural communication, God has poured out twenty years of extraordinary grace upon the world. And still, after all this time, prayer remains the central theme of the Medjugorje messages.

The village of Medjugorje is very much into the new century. Thousands of rooms for pilgrims are now available in Medjugorje. In comparison to possibly three tiny cafes operating in the first five years, there are now literally dozens of restaurants and cafes. Hotels abound, and souvenir shops number in the hundreds. Everything can be purchased in Medjugorje now. The world has surely arrived in Medjugorje in full force. During the anniversary week in June, every room was occupied and towns as far away as fifty miles were also filled to capacity. The harvest continues.

Yet, the holiness in the village has also increased. In fact, it far outstrips the influx of material trappings. This is borne out by the ever increasing number of pilgrims from countries throughout the world. Germany, Switzerland, Austria, Korea, South Africa and other countries are spawning pilgrimages in steady numbers. It is estimated that more than 30 million people have come to the village of apparitions.

And the Virgin implores us to carry on. In August 25, 2001, she gave this unique and powerful message: *Dear children! Today, I call all of you to decide for holiness. May for you, little children, always in your thoughts and in each situation holiness be in the first place, in work and in speech. In this way, you will also put it into practice. Little by little, step by step, prayer and a decision for holiness will enter into your family. Be real with yourselves and do not bind yourselves to material things but to God. And do not forget, little children, that your life is as passing as a flower. Thank you for having responded to my call.*

Unfortunately, the apparitions are still opposed, still rejected as an authentic gift of grace, especially by the local bishop of Mostar, Ratko Peric. The ongoing conflict between the bishop and the Franciscan priests has escalated to the point of smoldering confrontation. Duplicating an action of his predecessor, Bishop Peric chose the occasion of the confirmation ceremony at Medjugorje in July 2001 to publicly denounce the apparitions, deny their authenticity, and admonish religious and laity alike for their participation and support of them. His predecessor, Bishop Zanic, had done exactly the same thing during confirmation services in July 1986.

Making matters worse, in the early part of 2000, the bishop stripped Father Slavko Barbaric of his faculty of confession.

According to Father Slavko, who personally confided this action to me in August of that year, this action was taken without cause or explanation. No specific reason was given, nor was it a punishment for a stated infraction. Further, rumor had it that the bishop had ordered the transfer of Father Slavko to a place far away from Medjugorje. It was no secret that Father Slavko was the unofficial leader of many of the programs in Medjugorje stemming from the apparitions. Perhaps the bishop hoped that by removing Father Slavko he would decrease the interest of pilgrims and villagers alike. In any case, the order was to take effect November 26, 2000.

But, heaven intervened in a most astounding though poignant way. To the great sorrow of millions of Medjugorje followers, word spread within hours of the sudden, untimely death of Father Slavko on November 24, just two days before his dismissal and intended humiliation.

The fifty-four-year-old priest had led about seventy parishioners on the Way of the Cross as has been the parish's custom since the days of the war. It had rained on the way up, and as the group reached the summit, the sun came out. A beautiful rainbow appeared in the distance behind Saint James Church. Father Slavko finished the prayers, gave his blessing, and closed by uttering his final words on earth: "May the Gospa pray for us at the time of our death." As the group descended between the 13th and 14th stations, he suddenly sat down, then quietly stretched out on the ground and, within moments, was dead. He died at approximately 3:45 p.m. of an apparent heart attack.

It was a day of personal tears and sadness as I felt the loss of a dear friend and leader who was the active heart and soul of Medjugorje. But my grief and that of all followers of Medjugorje turned into unbounded joy the following day when visionary Marija received the November 25th monthly message from Gospa. In the last part of the message, the Virgin said: *I rejoice with you and I desire to tell you that your brother Slavko has been born into heaven and intercedes for you.*

Ironically, Father Slavko was first sent to the parish by Bishop Zanic in the spring of 1982 to help the bishop prove the apparitions were false. The highly educated Slavko reportedly returned to the bishop and stated simply that he believed that the Virgin was truly appearing. From that time on, he had served the parish faithfully. Almost every morning before six o'clock, he could be found in prayer on Mt. Krizevac. Before descending, he would gather bags of trash left by pilgrims atop the mountain. It was his special, self-imposed penance. He led numerous retreats and presentations in Medjugorje and conducted meetings on the theme of the Medjugorje events in many parts of the world.

There is little doubt in the hearts of those who knew this beloved priest personally, or through his numerous writings, projects, and lectures, that anything about the way he was taken from this earth was without purpose. Just as he served as an inspiration during his arduously active years as the spiritual leader of Medjugorje, he would now serve as an example of our reward for truly attempting to live the messages.

My association with Father Slavko began in June 1986, during my second trip to Medjugorje. A young, troubled sixteen-year-old Australian girl introduced us. Her name was Tanya. Suffering from drug addiction, she had been placed under Father Slavko's care by her family who had brought her to Medjugorje hoping for a cure and a conversion. I met Tanya and later was introduced to Father Slavko by her. He wanted to know who this American journalist was who had befriended his young charge. After a long interview with him where I related my own story of conversion through Medjugorje, he "approved" me as a friend of Tanya. Several days later, she asked Father Slavko to invite me into the apparition room on June 26, the day after the fifth anniversary of Medjugorje. It was my birthday—and this was a surprise birthday gift from Tanya. It was also the beginning of a long friendship with Father Slavko.

Tanya still lives in Australia and, after a long fifteen-year struggle, is at last cured of drug dependency. Father Slavko never gave up on Tanya. He stayed in touch with her. Today, she is trying to get her life together. In November 2001, she joined me and my pilgrimage in Medjugorje with her eleven-year-old daughter, Chantelle. Tanya had planned to stay only a few days and then go on to visit relatives from the region. But she ended up staying over two weeks and left Medjugorje with a fervent love of Jesus and a renewal of self esteem. I feel she will be all right with her guardian priest interceding for her in heaven!

Father Slavko's role as overseer of the apparition room was his toughest assignment. From the time it was in the small room in the rectory that also served as his bedroom, through the time in the choir loft, it was his daily responsibility to decide who would be allowed into the room during the apparition. It was an agonizing job that tore him apart each time: so many people in desperate need of special healing graces, so many priests, nuns and other clergy to be balanced with journalists, scientists, and those with special needs, like Tanya. Yet, he managed, through a combination of wisdom and toughness—and genuine humility.

I remember once going to confession to Father Slavko in one of the booths inside the church. I entered in awe and holy fear. I rushed through the formalities of the sacrament; he gave me absolution and I started to leave, relieved that it was over and knowing there was a line of people waiting. Within seconds, he smiled, asked how I was, and began talking about other things. Twenty minutes later I left the booth, cleansed of soul and uplifted in spirit. He had that way—sometimes so fierce and stoic, and at other times, just another human wanting to share a little of the everyday world.

That fierceness was most evident when pilgrims in their zeal would overwhelm him with praise or the taking of his picture. He disdained all such attention. During the youth festival in August 2000, I awaited Father Slavko late one afternoon near the church steps where he had told me to meet him. As he made his way toward me, he was suddenly attacked with an over-exuberance of fawning and praise by an Italian lady. She spoke a rapid string of Italian, grabbing his arm and asking to take his picture. He quickly jerked away and launched a wrathful barrage of his own Italian, telling the lady to stop treating him like a movie star—or words to that effect. He was so human—another reason everyone loved and admired him so much.

I was in Medjugorje in November, just two weeks before Father Slavko's untimely death. Alone on the last evening of our pilgrimage, I was just walking around enjoying the tranquility of the evening Croatian Mass. Father Slavko had been gone from Medjugorje for several days and I had not seen him since our arrival. Hearing a noise, I glanced to my left and there he was making his way toward the sacristy. Without a word he walked up to me, hugged me and asked how I was, gently patting the side of my face. I returned his hug and told him I was okay. "Good, I pray for you and your family," he said, and then quickly disappeared inside the sacristy to assist with the communion.

Father Slavko Barbaric was a man of few words, but every word was with purpose. I will always remember his last words to me, as well as the final prayer he spoke on Mt. Krizevac, a prayer surely meant for all the followers of Medjugorje. His final earthly gesture was a priestly blessing and a request for Our Lady to be with us at the hour of our death. This simple but meaningful act, along with this solemn prayer, bore witness to his whole Medjugorje ministry. It was and will remain a guiding light for all followers of Medjugorje.

．　．　．　．　．

Besides this you know what hour it is, how it is full time now for you to wake from sleep. For salvation is nearer to us now than when we first believed; the night is far gone, the day is at hand. Let us then cast off the works of darkness and put on the armor of light.　　　　　　　　　　　　　　　　　Romans 13:11-12

Chapter 31

September 11, 2001

The world has already given many meanings to the events of September 11, 2001, but for followers of Medjugorje, this day can only be understood in light of the spiritual situation of our times and the extended period of grace in which we are living. The causes of this tragedy, and the events that have followed it, are nothing other than an unfolding of the urgent warnings and hope-filled promises that the Blessed Virgin has made to her chosen visionaries over the last twenty years.

If the world needed a wake-up call, this was it. Four commercial airplanes containing innocent victims were turned into guided missiles by teams of suicidal, religious extremists. Two of the aircraft were deliberately crashed into the World Trade Center buildings in New York City, one following the other within minutes, creating billowing smoke and fire with debris raining down on the streets below. A short time later, another aircraft took a deliberate plunge into the Pentagon, while a fourth plummeted to the ground near Pittsburgh, Pennsylvania. This last was suspected of having another government site in mind as a target, though the heroism of its passengers seems to have cut that effort short.

The bustling activity of the nation ground to a halt while Americans listened or watched in stunned horror as news of the attack spread. By 10:00 a.m., the entire world knew that the nation of ultimate freedom and democracy had been severely wounded. For hours afterwards, televisions everywhere carried the replay of events that seemed more horrible than any story or film ever imagined. Not only buildings had crumbled to the ground, but the security that had surrounded a way of life was shattered beyond repair.

The attacks, while directly aimed at the United States, were not just against our country, but against all people who worshiped or believed differently than the attackers. It was done, according to the perpetrators, in the name of true Islam. The instigator of the attacks and leader of the suicide squad was purportedly Osama Bin Laden, an Islamic fundamentalist and known international terrorist who had been working from a secret site in Afghanistan with the support of the Taliban, the former governing body of that nation.

A twin-towered, New York City landmark, offices of worldwide economic and commercial corporations housing as many as 50,000 employees; and, the fortress of U. S. defense, the Pentagon, with more than 23,000 military and government employees, were deliberately chosen, symbolic targets of the first foreign attack on United States soil since the early 19th century. Shock was followed by fear and grief in the collective hearts of a people unaccustomed to such raw hatred and evil. The nation would never be the same again.

.   .   .   .   .

On the night of the attacks, Ivan's prayer group met in Medjugorje on the summit of Podbrdo Hill, the spot where the apparitions had begun. After a lengthy period of prayer, the Blessed Virgin appeared to Ivan; he commented afterward that he had never seen her looking so sad. According to some friends who were present, Ivan shared that Our Lady's sadness was the most important thing about this apparition, that except for her apparitions on Good Friday, she almost never appears sad. This evening she was sad, he added, because of her many children who had lost their lives in the tragedy in America.

The Virgin, as usual, blessed all present and prayed over everyone with her hands extended. She then gave this message: *MIR! MIR! MIR! Pray for peace! Pray together with your Mother for peace! Thank you, because you have responded to my call!* [emphasis added]

.   .   .   .   .

In the weeks following September 11, many people asked me if the attacks on the United States might not be one of the secrets of Medjugorje. I had to remind them that none of the secrets would occur until after the Virgin Mary had made her last appearance to the last remaining visionary or visionaries. It was, instead, a traumatic wake-up call to bring the entire world to full awareness of the need to return to moral law and order. In other words, to put God back in the first place in daily life.

As if to confirm this, the Blessed Virgin Mary gave this message at Medjugorje on September 25, 2001, just two weeks after the attack: *Dear children, also today I call you to prayer, especially when Satan wants war and hatred. I call you anew, little children: pray and fast that God may give you peace. Witness peace to every heart and be carriers of peace in this world with no peace. I am with you and intercede before God for each of you. And do not be afraid because the one who prays is not afraid of evil and has no hatred in the heart. Thank you for responding to my call* [emphasis added].

Even as I finish this update of Medjugorje's messages and impact, the world stands at the crossroads. Soon after the attacks, the United States, in conjunction with many other nations, launched air strikes against Afghanistan military and terrorist training sites. Within two weeks, it was evident that the extremist Islamic government would fall and a short time later, it did. Fear abounded as to what would happen next. Would the search for terrorists lead to an all-out war—a third world war between Islamic nations and the coalition of nations led by the United States?

Again, the answer would appear to be, no. The Virgin had stated in the early days of Medjugorje's apparitions that there would not be a third world war. However, the ageless war of good verses evil was definitely heightened to an extremely dangerous level. It remains heightened.

It is true that, in the first few hours following the attacks, many wondered if this were a sign of the end, the beginning of the apocalypse, the final battle between good and evil. The question was only natural given the enormity of the shock, the swiftness and magnitude of the devastation, and the worldwide implications that followed. But, if we accept the truth of the Medjugorje messages, we know that this event was not meant to open the last chapter on world history. It was, rather, a reason—another and, perhaps, most compelling reason—to listen to the words of the Lady from Heaven and live her messages.

The proof of this is there to be seen: from out of tragedy, a new hope has been born, a hope that has been the constant theme of Medjugorje: prayer. Americans, in an unprecedented way, have chosen to respond to this tragedy with prayer and compassion. This collective movement towards prayer is marked by freedom and humility, not panic or fear, and it is fueled by true compassion and pride in the new heroes of the country: the professional organizations of disaster relief, the firemen, the policemen, the emergency medical personnel, and countless others who simply came to help in any way possible.

For weeks following the attacks, voices raised in prayer rang out long and clear at every public gathering. Suddenly, no one was worrying about public prayers violating civil rights in schools or government buildings. Sports events and other normal activities stopped for at least a week and, once resumed, became staging grounds for displays of national spirit and prayer. A new sense of solidarity has bound Americans. We are rediscovering the high ideals that gave birth to our country; we are rededicating ourselves to the defense of life, freedom, and happiness. We are remembering God.

The United States has not entered this new spiritual awareness alone. In the hours immediately following the attacks, Americans were joined by millions from around the world who reached out with moral and material aids, recognizing that this crime was not against the United States per se, but against the very notion of freedom.

Vigils and memorials for the victims of the attacks were held at every corner of the globe while world leaders concurred in an unprecedented way to stand behind the United States in her pursuit of justice. Never before in the history of the world have so many people been united by one resolve: to protect the innocent by abolishing terrorism from the earth. Church leaders have taken the occasion to demonstrate an unprecedented solidarity on the fundamental dignity and rights of man and the true nature of a God who is love.

How can we explain such incredible fruits? Only by a grace gratuitously given and freely received. The tragedy was enormous, but not without meaning or value. The world has taken a new course and, almost despite itself, is responding to the Blessed Virgin's call.

. . . . .

In the midst of the immediate fallout of these events, I left for another trip to Medjugorje, arriving on October 9. Thousands were present; even Americans, who had been decreasing in numbers over the past two years, were there in moderate force. Those who had come were not afraid. Pilgrims filled every standing space in the church and around its grounds every day at every event. Prayer was continuous and focused on the present world crisis. The whole pilgrimage was marked by intense prayer and faith in the mercy and providence of God.

I returned home greatly calmed and sure that with such a response good would win out in the end. But my arrival back in the United States also brought me face to face with the continuing nature of the crisis. Mostly, I realized even more that my country had a desperate, urgent need to return to God.

Consider the morning of the attacks: headlines on prominent newspapers across the land reported the demand by scientific groups for more and broader stem cell research. Abortion rights were once again front-page news, as proponents sought more protection, more liberal laws of allowance and convenience. In short, America, the land of the greatest opportunity and freedom ever in the history of the world, was more focused on civil needs than on spiritual needs. We were wondering around in a darkness created by our own selfish interests.

Then, in an unforgiving burst of fire and destruction, America came face to face with her own soul. It could have been the moment for despair; it could have been the excuse to hurl ourselves and our world into a final catastrophe.

Yet, God in His mercy always shines a light in the midst of the worst darkness. That light—that grace—was particularly obvious in the events of September 11, 2001.

Taking into account the time of day, the number of people that would have been present in the World Trade Center and the Pentagon; and, the number of people on the airplanes, more than

74,000 people had been at risk in the terrorist attacks. Of that number, the official count of dead or presumed dead, as of January 2002, is a little less than 4,000. Of course, one death from such horror is too much. But imagine the toll of what could have been!

Americans seemed to grasp the miraculous intervention that had scaled down this tragedy. They certainly understood the meaning of the heroism and sacrifice of those who came to help and were themselves lost in the attempt. Astoundingly, though justice was called for, restraint also showed forth, and prayer was the common answer to an unthinkable evil.

A year later, the United States is once again, united. It is a country humbled, prayerful, and thankful to God for its blessings and freedoms. It is a country noticeably attempting to return to the ways of God. And once again, Satan has failed.

. . . . .

Have mercy upon us, O Lord, have mercy upon us. For we have had more than enough of contempt. Too long our soul has been sated with the scorn of those who are at ease, the contempt of the proud. Psalms 123:3-4

Epilogue:

Divine Mercy

After more than twenty years of wondrous apparitions and revealing messages, the final harvest nears conclusion. And, as the Blessed Virgin tells us, once the harvest is complete, humanity will live and worship God again as in ancient days. This theme resounds through all her apparitions on earth, especially in her messages at La Salette, Fatima, and to the Marian Movement of Priests.

According to the Blessed Virgin, the last phase of the harvest will be the fulfillment of the ten secrets—an event that will not take place until she has made her final apparition at Medjugorje. The revelation of the secrets will be a major piece in the mosaic of grace, one that will reflect the entirety of the apparition phenomenon and its manifestation of God's unconditional love. As we continue into the new century, there is a feeling that the time is near for the conclusion. It may occur at any time, though a realistic consideration of the factors involved would point to a time frame of about four years. That is my personal gut feeling.

I believe the last piece of the mosaic will be one of the first three secrets of Medjugorje. The Blessed Virgin has disclosed that these three secrets will be warnings to the world and proofs that the apparitions of Medjugorje are truly from God. According to Mirjana, who has been shown the first warning by vision (see chapter 15), there will be a major upheaval in a region of the world. The third warning, as we have seen, will be a permanent sign left at the spot where the Virgin first appeared. With these two secrets revealed to this extent, I believe the remaining piece of the mosaic lies in the second warning.

The entire phenomenon of Medjugorje is a gift of mercy. The last revelation, however, will be a final and definitive expression of Divine Mercy. It will be given through the Holy Spirit and will allow every living soul an opportunity to receive the grace of peace and happiness through belief in and acceptance of the ways of God.

Throughout the history of recorded apparitions, locutions, and other supernatural spiritual phenomena, there has been a consistent thread of prophecy that describes an interior "illumination" of the soul that will be experienced by every living human being at a designated time. Sometimes it is referred to as an illumination of the conscience. The illumination will occur at a time known only to God, and will suddenly permit every human being to see their soul exactly as God sees it.

Every sin committed will be visible to each individual soul, no matter how small or how great the sin; every good deed done will be visible, no matter how small or how great the deed. The world will literally stand still for a matter of time as this incomprehensible grace is given to all of humanity.

What happens following the illumination is then up to each individual. Those who believe in God will experience great good from it, while those without belief will suffer with the pain of truth. Some will die from the shock of seeing themselves as God sees them. The event will reveal to all faiths that God truly exists; it will be impossible to deny it after the illumination. Yet, each individual will still have the free will to accept or reject God. Unbelievably, there will be those who still reject Him.

There are many references to the final illumination in the texts of prophecies past and present, but we need look no further for corroboration than the locutions given to Father Stefano Gobbi, described in previous chapters. As we have seen, these messages strongly mirror the messages of the Blessed Virgin at Medjugorje. Appropriately, on Pentecost Sunday, June 4, 1995, the Virgin gave this powerful message confirming the illumination: *Tongues of fire will come down upon you all, my poor children, so ensnared and seduced by Satan and by all the evil spirits who, during these years, have attained their greatest triumph, and thus, you will be illuminated by this divine light, and you will see your own selves in the mirror of the truth and the holiness of God. It will be like a judgment in miniature, which will open the door of your heart to receive the great gift of Divine Mercy.* [emphasis added]

A year later, May 1996, Father Gobbi was given yet another message concerning this final mercy, one similar in tone: *Miraculous and spiritual tongues of fire will purify the heart and souls of all, who will see themselves in the light of God and will be pierced by the keen sword of his Divine Truth . . .*

Therefore, even at the eleventh hour, every person will be given the opportunity to respond to the Blessed Virgin Mary's call from Medjugorje. Clearly, her messages in Medjugorje are not about punishment, but about love: holy, divine love. They are an affirmation of the teaching of Holy Scripture, a proclamation of the "Good News" of Jesus Christ. The final harvest is not one of gloom and doom, but a joyous gathering together of God's children in an eternal embrace.

God has sent the Blessed Virgin in these times for all people, all who call themselves Christian, Jew, Muslim, Hindu—even those who call themselves atheists or non-believers. As always, she leads us in a gentle, motherly way, repeating over and over again the lessons her children need to learn.

Even into the third millennium, the Medjugorje message is basically the same as it has been since the first one given on June 25, 1981, as shown by her monthly message for January 25, 2002: *"Dear children! At this time while you are still looking back to the past year I call you, little children, to look deeply into your heart and to decide to be closer to God and to prayer. Little children, you are still attached to earthly things and little to spiritual life. May my call today also be an encouragement to you to decide for God and for daily conversion. You cannot be converted, little children, if you do not abandon sins and do not decide for love towards God and neighbor. Thank you for having responded to my call."*

May we be part of the Final Harvest of souls. May it be a harvest of great abundance.

. . . . .

Then I saw a new heaven and a new earth; for the first heaven and the first earth had passed away, and the sea was no more. And I saw the holy city, new Jerusalem, coming down out of heaven from God, prepared as a bride adorned for her husband; and I heard a great voice from the throne saying, "Behold, the dwelling of God is with men. He will dwell with them, and they shall be his people, and God himself will be with them; he will wipe away every tear from their eyes, and death shall be no more, neither shall there be mourning nor crying nor pain any more, for the former things have passed away." Revelation 21: 1-4

Selected Bibliography

Beyer, Richard J. *Medjugorje Day by Day*. Notre Dame, Indiana: Ave Maria Press, 1993.

Craig, Mary. *Spark from Heaven*. Notre Dame, Indiana: Ave Maria Press, 1988.

Delaney, John J. (editor) *A Woman Clothed with The Sun*. Garden City, New York: Image Books, 1960.

Sister Emmanuel. *Medjugorje, The 90's*. McKees Rocks, Pennsylvania: St. Andrew's Productions, 1997.

Gobbi, Stefano. *To the Priests, Our Lady's Beloved Sons*. St. Francis, Maine: The National headquarters of the Marian Movement of Priests in the United States of America, 1998.

Golob, D. R. *Live the Messages*. Harahan, Louisiana: 1987.

Manuel, David. *Medjugorje Under Siege*. Orleans, Massachusetts: Paraclete Press, 1992.

Pelletier, Joseph A., A.A. *The Queen of Peace Visits Medjugorje*. Worchester, Massachusetts: Assumption Publications, 1985.

_____. *The Sun Danced at Fatima*. Garden City, New York, Image Books, 1983.

Petrisko, Thomas W. *The Fatima Prophecies*. McKees Rock, PA: St. Andrew's Productions, 1998.

Weible, Wayne. *Letters From Medjugorje*. Orleans, Massachusetts: Paraclete Press, 1991.

_____. *Medjugorje: The Message*. Orleans, Massachusetts: Paraclete Press, 1989.

_____. *Medjugorje: The Mission*. Orleans, Massachusetts: Paraclete Press, 1994.

_____. *The Final Harvest.* Orleans, Massachusetts: Paraclete Press, 1999.

Words from Heaven. Birmingham, Alabama: Saint James Publishing, 1990.

To order additional copies of this book:

Please complete the form below and send to:

CMJ Marian Publishers
P.O. Box 661 • Oak Lawn, IL 60454
Toll free 888-636-6799
Call 708-636-2995 or fax 708-636-2855
Email: jwby@aol.com
www.cmjbooks.com

Name _____

Address _____

City _____ State _____ Zip _____

Phone (_____)_____

Final Harvest

	QUANTITY		SUBTOTAL
$14.95 x	_____	= $	_____
+ tax (for Illinois residents only)		= $	_____
+ 15% for S & H		= $	_____
TOTAL		= $	_____

Check # _____   ❏ Visa ❏ MasterCard
                        ❏ Discover Card ❏ American Express

Card # _____

Signature _____